Orange Alert

Also by Debra L. Brown

Changes

Also by Debra L. Brown and David A. H. Brown

Governance Gone Global

Looking for Leaders

Planning to Prevail

Replacing a Few Good Men: The Changing Face of Canada's Boards

Success in the Boardroom

When Leaders Serve

Where Good Governance Begins

Women on Boards: Not Just the Right Thing ... But the Bright Thing

Orange Alert

Learning from Stories and Reflections of September 11th

Debra L. Brown
And
David A H. Brown

Note for Librarians: a cataloguing record for this book that includes Dewey Decimal Classification and US Library of Congress numbers is available from the Library and Archives of Canada. The complete cataloguing record can be obtained from their online database at:
www.collectionscanada.ca/amicus/index-e.html
ISBN 1-4120-3717-4
Printed in Victoria, BC, Canada

TRAFFORD

Offices in Canada, USA, Ireland, UK and Spain

This book was published *on-demand* in cooperation with Trafford Publishing. On-demand publishing is a unique process and service of making a book available for retail sale to the public taking advantage of on-demand manufacturing and Internet marketing. On-demand publishing includes promotions, retail sales, manufacturing, order fulfilment, accounting and collecting royalties on behalf of the author.

Book sales for North America and international:
Trafford Publishing, 6E–2333 Government St.,
Victoria, BC V8T 4P4 CANADA
phone 250 383 6864 (toll-free 1 888 232 4444)
fax 250 383 6804; email to orders@trafford.com

Book sales in Europe:
Trafford Publishing (UK) Ltd., Enterprise House, Wistaston Road Business Centre,
Wistaston Road, Crewe, Cheshire CW2 7RP UNITED KINGDOM
phone 01270 251 396 (local rate 0845 230 9601)
facsimile 01270 254 983; orders.uk@trafford.com

Order online at:
www.trafford.com/robots/04-1545.html

10 9 8 7 6 5 4 3 2

Dedicated to the Canadians Who Lost Their Lives

Michael G. Arczynski, Vancouver, 1956

Garnet "Ace" Bailey, 1948

David Michael Barkway, 1967

Ken Basnicki, 1952

Jane S. Beatty, 1948

Joseph K. Collison, 1951

Cynthia (Cindy) Connolly, 1961

C. Arron Dack, 1961

Frank Joseph Doyle, 1962

Christine Egan, 1946

Michael Egan, 1950

Albert Alfy William Elmarry, 1970

Meredith Emily June Ewart, 1972

Peter Adam Gad Feidelberg, 1967

Ralph Gerhardt, 1967

Leroy W. Homer Jr., 1965

Soo-jin (Stuart) Lee, 1970

Mark Ludvigsen, 1969

Bernard Mascarenhas, 1947

Colin R. McArthur, 1949

Mike A. Pelletier, 1965

Donald Arthur Robson, 1949

Ruffino (Roy) F. Santos III, 1964

Vladimir Tomasevic , 1965

Chantal Vincelli, 1963

Debbie Williams, 1966

About the Book

Three years after the searing events of September 11th, 2001, we pause to remember the life-changing learnings, to honour the Canadian victims, and to look forward with hope and strength.

This book, a tribute to the Canadians who lost their lives in the twin towers that day, recounts the uniquely Canadian aspects of this world-scale story, through interviews, reflections and poems from Canadians from all walks of life.

Read touching and heart-wrenching poems and reflections from elementary school children; remember your recollections of that day alongside John Manley, Rita MacNeil, Peter Dey and other Canadian leaders; reflect on your learnings and changes as you hear firsthand experiences of Ground Zero from journalists and disaster relief workers.

These stories and reflections run the gamut of our collective journey that began on September 11th. Beginning with disbelief and overwhelming grief, moving through acts of sacrifice, courage and hospitality, our journey of healing and hope is ongoing and still palpable. Through all the sadness, fear and darkness, above all these stories are about how good prevailed on September 11th, and how good can prevail if we make the right choices today.

Table of Contents

Chapter I

Orange Alert

Much has happened in the months and even years since the terrorist attacks of September 11th 2001. We have watched as the war on terror has been fought in Afghanistan and then in Iraq. We have seen the terrible injuries and deaths of soldiers and civilians alike in these conflicts. Leaders have debated and led, followers have bravely and faithfully served. We have witnessed heartache and tragedy mixed with joy and triumph and spiders being chased from their holes.

But have we truly learned the lessons of September 11th? Will the Orange Alerts of today elevate to Red or subside permanently to a state of prolonged peace? We are the only ones who can determine that future. In September 11th, we have been given the opportunity to learn and reflect, to find the way to the future that is marked by understanding, peace and hope. This book is intended to help in some small measure to remind us how to find the way.

This book is a collection of interviews conducted during the initial six months following the September 11th attacks. The stories and memories reflect the freshness of emotion we all felt during that period. We have chosen to publish these stories now, three years later, as a reminder to the nation. A reminder that we must not forget the terror of that day, the lessons we learned about ourselves, the strength that we found in our faith and in others, and most importantly, we must never forget those who died.

September 11th has affected me progressively, in different ways. For the first few months, I was incredibly sad. It was difficult to focus on work or priorities. I went through the motions, continuing to fly almost weekly–I wasn't afraid–yet I wasn't the same.

But I was drawn—am drawn even today—to TV, to CNN; it's the first thing I do now after my prayer and devotional time each morning. Before September 11th, I read the headlines in the local newspaper and maybe watched the late news on TV. After September 11th, I was filled with an overwhelming sense of sadness and concern for the world and its future – it is more important to me now what is happening in the world around me.

Then one day I gave myself a shake. I needed to DO something. Firefighters responded by providing relief services and fighting fires, Customs officials by securing our borders, soldiers and sailors by jumping to our defence, government leaders through political action and new policy, children by collecting pennies and sending them where any help was needed. What was I uniquely equipped to do, to respond, to help? What was my unique calling?

David and I spend most of our time researching, reading, writing, speaking and teaching. Surely we could channel those gifts into creating a book, uniquely Canadian, as a tribute and testimony to those Canadians who died on that terrible day.

Just as we often overlook those who died at the Pentagon or on the planes—people like Todd Beamer and so many others—we also often overlook those from so many countries who died. This was and continues to be a world event. In fact, there were 26 Canadians who died in the September 11th attacks. So we sought out a number of Canadians to tell their story, because of the 26 who could not. In a way, the living are continuing the stories of those who died, speaking for them and in tribute to them.

We have reached out across Canada and spoken with people from various walks of life and professions. We spoke with children, students, adults, professionals, politicians and emergency workers, among others. We listened to their stories. Their's are stories of emotion and memories burned deeply within them. They are also stories of lessons learned and commitments to the future. We know they will touch you as intimately as they did us. Their stories helped us to heal and to act and so we moved from shock, to action, to hopefulness, to understanding, to change. Our hope is that you will too.

Chapter 2

Living Out Our Values

John Manley, PC, MP: A Politician

John Manley was the Member of Canada's Parliament for Ottawa South since being first elected in 1988. On September 11th, 2001, he was Canada's Foreign Minister. On September 12th, he began to Chair a Special Cabinet Committee on Security and Anti-Terrorism. He then served as Deputy Prime Minister and has subsequently stepped down from elected service. Mr. Manley was Time Magazine's Canadian "Newsmaker of the Year" in 2001, the year we are remembering. In this candid interview John shares with us where he was when he found out and how our government responded in those first few hours of crisis.

Everybody's lives changed that day, many in frustrating ways, some in subtle ways, always in uncertain ways. The thing that stands out in my mind, though, the thing that makes me proudest to be Canadian, is ordinary people living Canadian values without a thought for themselves, their own safety, their material possessions: they just acted. That is truly what values are: something that you hold so deeply, when called upon, you just know the right thing to do, and you do it.

Of course, September 11th completely upset my life. One day I was in Europe meeting with European foreign ministers planning for the G-8 summit. The next day I was in charge of a

Cabinet Committee charged with leading our nation's response to security and terrorism concerns.

In some ways, though, I feel very privileged. I can get up in the morning and go into the office and work directly on initiatives that deal with September 11th and its aftermath, and I know that many Canadians feel frustrated that they don't feel they are able to make a difference. Yet it is what we each do every day, and what each Canadian did that week, that ultimately makes the difference and communicates our values to the whole world.

The Air Canada Boeing 747 was a few hours out of Frankfurt when a flight attendant leaned over me and quietly asked me to go with him. He took me up to the second floor deck where a second crew member was waiting. Between the two of them, they gave me what at first sounded to me a confused story about planes going into buildings.

My initial thought was that it had been an accident.

"No, no," was their response. This was no accident. They handled things very professionally, deciding not to alarm the other passengers, finding me a seat on the flight deck with the pilots. They had never experienced this before, but they knew what to do, and they did it.

They handed me a headset and plugged me in to BBC radio, whose correspondents were reporting from the scene in New York City and Washington. Together we sat in silence as the news got worse, and as Tony Blair made his first statement.

For all their efforts, though, radio just couldn't do it justice; you could not conceive of what had happened until you actually *saw* the TV footage of the planes hitting the buildings, and of the buildings collapsing.

They tried to connect me with the Canadian government by satellite phone. I had to find out what I could do, what the government was doing, to fulfil our responsibilities. We did get through briefly, but all the lines were clogged with callers frantic from news from both sides of the Atlantic.

The pilots remarked how silent things were in the air; usually there was a constant chatter going back and forth between flight crew and ground controllers, but now there was nothing but curt instructions and clipped acknowledgements. U.S. air space had been closed, and planes were being diverted by controllers elsewhere. Transatlantic flights that were still far enough from North America were ordered to turn around and return to Europe. Ours was the last flight let through to North America, not because of me or anyone else, we just happened to be on the cusp, just far enough from Europe to make more sense to keep flying on.

We landed at Toronto around 4:00 p.m. Pearson airport looked deserted; the few planes that had been diverted there were already long parked and emptied. There were no line-ups at Customs or luggage. (There was one normal thing, though: one of my bags didn't come off the carousel, and indeed it took quite some time to find its way home to Canada!)

The Airport Authority management arranged an office for me and I was able to secure a line to the Prime Minister. He gave me a quick briefing on what had been done already and to go into action.

We didn't know if there were other terrorists, or other potential risks that we needed to deal with. All of that had to be put into play right away. The Prime Minister gave me a quick rundown on all that had been accomplished already. The air space closed, except for receiving the planes that were diverted, and various defence and security operations that were in place on an emergency basis.

What I found out was mind-boggling but heartening. 240 flights with 33,000 airline passengers had been diverted to Canada in the minutes following the September 11th attacks.

I like to think that, after the emergency workers at New York City, Washington and Pennsylvania, Canadians were the first people to respond to September 11th. Defence, RCMP, air traffic controllers, Customs people, airport staff, ordinary Canadians from coast to coast, galvanized into action without a single rehearsal, handling the next few days with professionalism and humanity.

The Minister of Transport sent a plane down to take me back to Ottawa that evening. I tried first to reach Colin Powell, the U.S. Secretary of State, but he too had been flying back from a foreign meeting—in Peru. I reached him early the next day, and then we began to plan the reaction.

We certainly had a heightened level of anxiety among Canadians, but the anxiety of our neighbours was of course even higher, and one of my immediate tasks as Foreign Minister was to help our American neighbours.

In those early days, we had to deal with the widespread myth than two of the terrorists had crossed from Canada. It had no basis in truth, but it was repeated at high levels of the U.S. government. I think it must have begun with the news—and video frames—of two hijackers boarding a plane in Portland, Maine. Because of how close Portland is to Canada, many people assumed they'd entered from here, although it turned out they'd come up from Florida. Alongside this myth, there were valid concerns that we had to address to reduce the likelihood that terrorists could cross into the U.S. across our border. I didn't want to see our border close for a prolonged period. We had to act, our responsibility was to deal with both the perceptions and the realities of the new situation.

The U.S. needed assurance of our solidarity and of their security, and of course we ensured the appropriate response.

I say "appropriate" but you know in this case—as so often in life—the "right" thing for us to do was also the "smart" thing. The openness of our border is a vital economic factor, and its security must be of paramount importance to both countries. That's a lesson in values: doing the right thing is often also the smart thing. But you don't do it because it's smart, you do it because it's right.

Everybody's lives changed on September 11th. Suddenly I was in charge of a special committee of cabinet on security and antiterrorism, trying to deal with the response the government had to show to the events.

The big story, to me, though, is how Canadians responded on September 11th, the massive humanitarian effort. I heard so many stories that I was tremendously moved.

One planeload of passengers was so touched by the hospitality of a small village in Newfoundland that, on returning home, these strangers who had never met before decided to start a scholarship fund and raised $38,000 for young students from the village.

I spoke with Senator Cantwell from Washington, whose daughter was returning from a once-in-a-lifetime trip to Japan on September 11th. Her plane was diverted to Yellowknife, and her experiences there — including a caribou barbecue — completely eclipsed her Asian trip. She will be forever grateful to her hosts and treasure those unforgettable, unplanned days.

Another planeload was housed in the beautiful Annapolis Valley of Nova Scotia. Their experience was so positive that they made and hung a banner on their departure, reading:

Took off from New York and landed in Heaven

September 11th is one of those dates that a whole generation will remember where it was. I will never forget sitting in that plane, feeling a combination of dumbfoundedness and disbelief, just as I will never forget where I was on November 22nd, 1963, when President Kennedy was shot.

I will also never forget what it felt and sounded like on that gorgeous September day when hundreds of thousands of people stood shoulder-to-shoulder together on Parliament Hill and sang the U.S. national anthem. The Prime Minister had been strongly advised to hold the service inside, in a church or meeting hall, but he decided not to. The September 14th event was a powerful experience, simple, short and moving. Above all, it reflected the solidarity of the people of Canada at that moment, that week, setting aside differences and concentrating on acting together according to their values.

September 11th was a signal, loud and clear, that our world will never be the same again. Never again will we be able to allocate our resources as we did before. We understand this, but it is disappointing, that concerns about security will cost us all, money, time and comfort. This burden of reality will stay with us.

We have learned that our planet is a very small place, and not as benign a place as many of us thought it was or wish it were—if we did take comfort in that before, we cannot now. We've learned that there is a price to a free and open society—someone has to protect that. Our police, military and security forces are necessary to protect the kind of openness we expect and value.

Those of us who embrace these values need to recognize, too, that we need to work tirelessly to resolve the issues that are out there, that give some people the notion that their life is better used by committing suicide than by trying to work towards justice in another way. I think many of us have trouble with the fact that these men were skilled, intelligent, some of them university-educated, married, older . . . whatever it was that convinced them that they should die for a cause, is something we must address if we want the world to be a safer place. We cannot cease working to convince them and assure them that their lives have value being lived, not ended. That's what living out our values requires of us.

Drawing By: Joyce Wong, 13 years old, Bayview Hill Elementary School, Richmond Hill, Ontario

Chapter 3

Keeping the Peace

John Leontowicz: A Police Chief

John Leontowicz is the Chief of Police in LaSalle, an Ontario municipality adjacent to Windsor and just across the St. Clair River from Detroit, Michigan. John has served in policing for over 25 years, including a significant span with the Royal Canadian Mounted Police.

Keeping the peace is more of a calling than a vocation, and certainly more of a journey than a destination. It is a journey with ups and downs, long quiet straight-aways punctuated by sudden and bizarre twists and turns.

One of those bizarre twists came right out of the blue on September 11th, 2001. That morning found me working at my desk, putting the finishing touches on a counter terrorism policy for our force and community. Not that counter-terrorism was foremost in our minds, but my background in the RCMP had etched awareness of the scale of threat perhaps more acutely in my mind, and the time had arrived for codifying and strengthening some of our precautionary measures.

"Chief, you'd better have a look at this" my secretary announced. Together we walked into the lunchroom to join others gasping at the TV broadcast of one of the twin towers in New York City burning. While we watched, a second plane flew into the other tower.

We knew right away it was a terrorist attack, although had no idea who was responsible. At first, we thought it might be people aligned with those responsible for the Oklahoma City bombing—U.S. domestic terrorists.

Our nature and training as keepers of the peace focus us on identifying the perpetrators, but that morning it was impossible not to be overwhelmed with thoughts about the victims. My heart went out to those innocent people who had absolutely no idea what was happening to them.

Right now, however, there wasn't anything we could do for those folks, but there was a whole community that we had sworn to protect. In my experience as a police officer, incidents usually start at their worst and gradually get better as emergency workers get things under control and order is restored. On September 11th, it just kept getting worse. The first plane, the second plane, the Pentagon, the Pennsylvania crash, the first tower down, the second tower down—even as more emergency workers poured in to help, they had no idea it was going to keep getting worse.

We had no idea where and when these attacks were going to end. LaSalle is right on the border with Michigan, just a few hundred yards from the busiest border crossing in the country, the tunnel and bridge linking Detroit and Windsor. Within a few kilometers from our police station lie GM Place, major office towers, manufacturing plants, the Fermi 2 nuclear facility, as well as one of the largest Muslim communities on the continent. Even though the overwhelming majority would condemn these violent acts, how small a number financially contributed to extremist terrorists? How many were affiliated with Al Qaeda? Al Qaeda is not just comprised of Palestinians and Afghanis, but includes Arabs, Africans, indeed members from many different nationalities. There could easily have been 10,000 in place readied to all attack at once on September 11th.

Communications with national and provincial authorities were not very good for the first 48 hours after the attacks. Each community acted to protect its citizens. I picked up the phone to the Mayor, who also serves as Chair of the Police Services Board, and we initiated an emergency measures meeting. In a matter of minutes, we linked up with the Deputy Mayor, Chief Administrative Officer and Fire Chief to direct steps to be taken to protect the community.

Windsor declared an emergency, largely due to the bridge and tunnel, where security was put on the highest alert status. If someone wanted to cross between Canada and Detroit, the river would now be their natural choice, and its closest point was at our doorstep, LaSalle.

Our emergency measures plan moved into effect. Active police and fire services were put on alert, patrols and security at key sites heightened. Investigative teams, police and fire watches were put on standby in case of an incident. Keeping the peace is more than reacting—it means putting into action years of anticipating, planning and preparation. You have to be ready even for the unexpected.

The sheer magnitude and scale of September 11th dwarfed everything before and after. We thought Oklahoma City was the worst thing we'd ever see. Over the years, I'd given a lot of thought to terrorism, but now as police chief, we were no longer discussing the possibility of terrorist acts. We had to treat every threat as real. The Salvation Army called us, reporting a ticking sound coming from one of their large metal donation bins that sounded like a time bomb. We dispatched the bomb squad and treated the threat as a potential terrorist attack. It turned out that someone had thrown in a battery-operated power toy as a donation, and its switch had been knocked on by the impact inside the bin. After the anthrax attacks, I had to draft a policy dealing with precautions in case of an unknown foreign substance with the power to wipe out the entire police force. We even had a number of anthrax hoaxes in our own community.

As emergency workers, the most lasting and deepest impact has been the firefighters and police officers who lost their lives. So many of them went up into the second tower to help people, not knowing that the first tower's fire was a terrorist attack, then the second tower was the first to collapse. Five hundred emergency workers killed, trying to save innocent lives. Nothing like this had ever happened before. When we lose one firefighter or police officer in the line of duty, it has a dramatic effect. When Canada lost 4 soldiers in a bombing accident, it was a major national tragedy. Can you imagine the impact of losing 500 emergency workers at one time?

We were all personally touched by the video narrated by Robert de Niro following emergency workers on September 11th into the Towers. We could easily picture our own team in such an impossible and confusing position. These were truly our brothers and sisters. From a few days after the attacks, we'd been in touch with U.S. police about taking a contingent of police from Canada to New York City for a memorial service. Literally thousands of police and firefighters from across Canada stood ready to attend, but the services had been smaller and private, in keeping with the wishes of those on the scene. Keeping the peace calls for teamwork, for solidarity, sometimes for superhuman effort and bravery. It has to be a calling, not just a job.

I don't know if it's the beginning of a trend, or just a blip, but since September 11th, there has been a larger number of police officers killed on duty in Canada—in Manitoba, Saskatchewan, Alberta, B.C., Quebec, Belleville, Toronto . . . I don't recall ever seeing this many. Perhaps the world is a more dangerous place to live in these days, and those charged with keeping the peace are on the front lines of that danger. Yet even these tragedies are overshadowed still by September 11th and consequent events in Afghanistan and the Middle East. What is going on in the world is in everybody's face.

As individuals, we have been woken and shaken up, right across North America—I don't think it will ever return to normal one hundred per cent. In the past, we were so wrapped up in our local problems, and treated international incidents, like bombings of U.S. embassies and Israel, as remote—like TV shows or movies.

Of course my own family was very shocked at September 11th. At first they watched the TV and thought it was a TV hoax, like the movie "Wag the Dog"—for a moment only. We do keep traveling, but now I'm on constant surveillance. I used to sit in airports and on planes reading magazines. Now I am watching, acutely aware of my circumstances and surroundings. We used to leave the door unlocked when we're home, now we lock the doors. If the kids are home alone, they don't answer the doorbell. We must accept the possibilities every day now. Keeping the peace means taking precautions, staying vigilant and never taking peace for granted.

LaSalle's new counter-terrorism policy was fine-tuned and out by the end of that long day on September 11th. It was influenced as much by my years in the RCMP as by the events leading to September 11th. The closer you get to terrorism, the more aware you are of the real possibilities of terrorists and what is available to them. The policy encourages uniformed officers to take nothing for granted, to be vigilant and observant, to pass along anything suspicious to the right authority immediately. While I hope and pray it will never happen in our community, I remind my force that it was a single Customs officer's vigilance and awareness at a Canadian/U.S. border ferry crossing that stopped Ressam and the Millennium bombing plot. Keeping the peace is everybody's business, as civilians and uniforms alike form the "thin blue line" to establish and restore peace.

Drawing By: Brittany Kleist, Grade 5, St. Mary's School, Goderich, Ontario

Chapter 4

Pennies for Peace

Sharon Martin: A Teacher

Sharon Martin is an elementary school teacher in Warburg, Alberta. She teaches a Grade 4 class, is a wife and a mother of two. The Warburg community helped Sharon celebrate her son's 7th birthday on April 4th, 2002.

I guess September 11th would have had a dramatic effect on me even if I hadn't personally experienced a seemingly pointless tragic event in my life. But as things turned out, the ground was being prepared for us, pointing us in a direction of clarity and meaning.

Before children, I was extremely career-minded. I thought that when I had children, I would promptly return to work. I wouldn't even entertain the idea of staying home. I loved my work, and I just knew that I would be much happier there than at home.

Being able to have children turned out not to be an easy task, though, and by thirty-five I had basically given up hope of having a family. Then, as life would often have it, when we least expect it, I found out we were finally expecting!

When our son was 7 weeks old, my mom, our son and myself were involved in a pedestrian accident. The driver of a car lost control and ploughed into the three of us.

Fortunately, no one was killed. However, our healthy son sustained severe brain damage. The first reports from his health care providers held out no hope for him to live.

I became aware as to how precious a second is then, and how one second can change your life forever. My outlook on life and its value changed drastically. Personal goals such as the completion of our new house had been put on the back burner, and that was seven years ago.

Our son finally scribbling on our walls became a giant celebration. His first jump off of the coffee table was a celebration. Everything that I was not going to allow while raising children became a celebration! Things that so many take for granted, are not in our household.

I realize that, in a way, this previous experience allowed me, after the numbness started leaving me, to be more reflective, compassionate, loving, and to search for the thread that would guide us to a positive aspect in this tragedy. This may seem strange to you; however, I have had to learn this personally: if you can't find the positive thread, you cannot learn from such a horrific experience and help others who have not had to experience something so devastating.

On September 11th, I was at home getting ready for work, still in my housecoat, curling my hair and eating breakfast. The news was on in the background on TV, and so I heard of a plane hitting one of the twin towers in New York City. I paused momentarily, but thought I must have heard wrong and kept going. Then I saw the images on the TV screen, above the banner "Breaking News."

"Oh my God." I said it aloud and I said it in my heart.

My first reaction was disbelief. I needed to talk to someone. My husband had already left for work, so I picked up the phone and called my dad. I'm not sure why, other than I knew he would be up—he was in the thick of harvesting—and I knew he would be interested. My mom and dad are "snowbirds": they go to the U.S. every winter.

"Is this really happening?" I asked my dad. "Could such a thing happen in the U.S.?"

I have a forty-five minute drive in the country to the rural school where I teach, typically forty-five minutes to relax, reflect and prepare for the day. This forty-five minute drive was unlike any other. Every combine in the fields stood idle, even though it was a beautiful dry morning. I listened intently to the radio as more news poured in. The Pentagon was hit and on fire. I called the school office, urging them to turn on the one TV in the school, a little set in the staff room.

Initially, I saw this as an adult story, that wouldn't interest the kids. That myth was shattered moments after getting out of my car in the parking lot at school, when one child came running up to me.

"Mrs. Martin, will my dad have to go to war now?"

From that moment on, I realized that this was an everybody-story, kids definitely included. The kids wanted the radio kept on in the classroom, and wouldn't go out for recess. The whole class wanted to know everything, and to talk about it all day long in class. I didn't know what else to teach, I was numb to everything else.

So we did talk, and I kept an eye on them, for different people deal in different ways with tragic events. We had been learning about maps and scales, so we gathered around the class map of North America. We located New York City, and Washington, and worked out how far away they are from Warburg. I put my little finger on Warburg and, using the same hand, put my thumb on New York City. The kids were surprised at just how near they really are.

The world is much smaller than we once thought. Other people's actions do affect others. One action in New York affected everyone in Warburg. I encouraged the kids to find positive value and learnings, to understand differences and hate, but to try to fathom them and deal with hate.

Four girls needed more: they needed to be able to *see* what was happening as well. I asked a teacher's assistant, who was also the mom of one of the girls, to stay with them in the staff room and watch their reactions while we let them watch events unfold on TV.

After school, and for days afterwards, I was on the phone calling parents of kids in my class, especially the ones who seemed most upset and worried.

Here, I realized, despite the horrific events, was a great learning opportunity, a teachable moment, a single event that we had all witnessed, and that every one of us, parents, children and teachers, wanted to—needed to—talk about. Those kinds of moments don't happen often in life, but when they do, you make the most of them.

The next day, kids brought in articles from newspapers and wanted to talk. From that day on, I have been much more open and flexible with their curriculum. We talk about current events, about September 11th, whenever they want to.

Not every one wants to talk, though; it soon became clear that some kids were just too upset to talk. We gave them the opportunity to meet together separately from the rest of class, with teachers' assistants staying with and helping them. We may not have been prepared to be counselors, but sometimes events require us to be.

The following day, the four girls who had expressed the most interest came up to me. They had decided they had to *do* something more. So they started collecting pennies for peace. It began with the four of them, they led, and their parents and I gave them support when they needed it.

"Pennies 4 Peace" has been going ever since. It has grown from these four girls to our whole class, from our one school to schools everywhere, thanks to the Internet and the communications in our small world, sending pennies to us in Warburg.

Our Superintendent of Schools came to meet with us. He said that many of us, including himself, had regarded pennies as a useless coin. A coin that either got lost on the street or tossed into an old jar. Yet putting them all together did make a difference, because within two months, the students counted out $6,000.00!

The Superintendent said that next time someone hands him a penny, he will think twice about it. Although small in currency value, it is very valuable when added together with other pennies.

Since September 11th, different events have brought back those feelings all over again.

Remembrance Day was one. Remembering those veterans who had given their lives for our freedom, and those serving even now overseas to protect us, suddenly had greater meaning than ever before.

Our grade 4 class had been trying to find threads that would interest students in the primary grades. Often it's hard for younger children to connect to events like September 11th. On Remembrance Day, then, our class realized that Winnie the Pooh, his connection to the war and a Canadian soldier, was the perfect thread. They talked with the primary grades about Winnie the Pooh and it worked.

Those who liked math found a way to involve it in the class project. Since Sears had agreed to match our donated pennies, it was a good chance each day for multiplication practice, and when that got too easy, the kids started to figure out the number of pennies it would take to add up to the perimeter of the gym!

One day will stand out for us. Students observed "your eyes got huge and big" one afternoon while the lawn was being cut. The motor sounded to me like a plane, and everyone in the class went deadly quiet right away. The healing process is a journey of many small steps.

We had all shared an experience, and were all on the same journey of healing. As we watched how the class knitted together to accomplish a goal with the pennies, we saw the value of an individual person, be it a firefighter in New York or a Grade 4 student in Warburg.

Each one of us is important. Each person will be valued for their own contributions. Each person—regardless of age, colour, or background—can make a great impact in the world. We now say in our class, "never underestimate what a small child can do." They too have worries and concerns well beyond their own family and school, and they can affect outcomes thousands of miles away.

Canada is like that, too. A small country in influence, on the fringes of the world, with the huge United States just next door. Yet we can make a difference, we can take steps to lead other nations, to add other voices to ours. We have great value.

My son is turning seven years old, and each second I have with him is precious. Something tragic happened in his life, and I could have focused on blame. We found out that the driver of the car that hit us was an older lady whose husband was dying of cancer. She was so worried and detached, that she had a black-out and so lost control of the car. How can I blame her? After the accident, I had memory lapses myself. I could see myself in her place, so all I could do now was to find the positive value, to learn and keep on living, treasuring each second.

Bad things will happen in this world and in our personal lives. Care for people beyond your own circle. Actually, expand your circle of care to encompass others. These are some of the Grade 4 lessons of September 11th.

Our slogan during the Pennies 4 Peace campaign has come to describe what we mean:

We are all like pennies . . .
Standing alone we are
Sometimes forgotten,
But add us all together and
We CAN make a difference!

Drawing by: Amy Mosicki, Grade 5, Warburg School, Warburg Alberta

Chapter 5

A Father's Love

Mike Woodard: A Father

Mike Woodard is a father of four who lives in Abbotsford, British Columbia. His work with youth and ministry co-ordination takes Mike to university and college campuses across Canada as well as in developing countries throughout Asia and Latin America.

I walked into McDonalds and someone asked, "did you see that?" I turned around to look at the television just in time to see the World Trade Center collapse in a cloud of dust.

My first impression was that it must be a movie preview, for something like "Die Hard 5", or maybe footage from the Discovery Channel on the demolition of buildings.

Then, truth came drifting in. This was real, this was the World Trade Center. This wasn't a terrible accident, I discovered, but an orchestrated attack. The tears beginning to stream down my cheeks, I stood in disbelief, thinking, "NO, this cannot be happening . . . those buildings are full of people . . . moms, dads, sons, daughters, sisters, brothers . . ."

I wanted to weep for all those that had lost their lives and the families that would never be the same again.

My eyes were pooling with tears, but I had to control myself; after all I was in the middle of McDonalds, full of moms, dads, sons, daughters, sisters, brothers . . . families.

Then the questions came: why? Who? What will happen next? It was hard to think of anything else. So many stories flew around about the events of that morning. What really happened? Is there any safe spot in the world? What kind of hate would motivate someone to do this? Someone asked: "Is this the beginning of the end?"

Around campuses, people immediately became very reflective, asking deep questions. What will the future hold? Many students began to question what they had put their confidence in—financial security, personal stability, physical safety. Yet there must be something there, something beyond these, to hold onto.

I work with a lot of professors. One told me once that he was convinced that we would reach utopia through education and technology. "We can do almost anything we put our minds to. After all, we are the most educated, advanced generation that has ever lived." I wonder what he was thinking on September 11th.

I spoke with another professor in New York City. He had been there when the towers were built; he had watched as the months passed, and the twin towers rose slowly. He had been there too to see them come down in a matter of minutes. Here it was, the World Trade Center, a symbol of man's accomplishment and sophistication, with all the things that were housed in these two towers, crumbling down. Truly a humbling thing to think about.

We were all gripped with the brevity of life—we may never get another chance to talk with people we love about the eternal. This was a wake-up call, that the sum total of all the things we can accomplish is just a veneer—what lies beneath that, is it a solid foundation or rotting wood that would collapse all around you? What will last? What will fail?

As the days passed, the questions continued.

My youngest daughter came home from school totally overwhelmed by the amount of school time filled with discussion of September 11th and the events of that day. I was in third grade when President Kennedy was shot—I still remember seeing the images on TV that day from Dallas—it shaped my whole view of politics, of the presidency, of love and hate . . . it will be interesting to see how the young people of today will be shaped by September 11th.

Even months later, I am surprised how dramatically it affects me.

In small ways. I didn't watch much TV before September 11th. We didn't even have cable. The cable company offered us a free trial offer just a few days before. Often since then I've found myself glued to TV news 'til late into the night—way too late—trying to find the answers to what happened, and to tie it all together.

In big ways, too. Waves of emotion still wash over me, the same sense of mourning as when my father died. Yes, I am thinking of the impact on the families of those who died that day, but more than that, I am mourning the death of innocence.

Today I ask, "How could someone have so much hate to kill thousands of innocent people?" I don't get on a flight without looking around wondering if someone is so full of hate that they might want to kill me and the others on the flight. People will never be able to fix themselves; we just can't do it.

"God, how could this be happening? Why?" I pictured God with tears in His eyes as He observed the result of some of His children rejecting His love . . .

I know my kids are going to travel the world—as a father, I know what dangers exist—as Canadians, they may now be targeted. Here was a wild card event that mixed fantasy and reality—something from a novel—at first we reject it as fiction, then once we accept it, we wonder what else could happen. It is no longer a question of *if* the next strike will happen, but when, where and how? We face together the cold reality of what the rest of the world has had to face for a long time. The world is smaller; we are strangely closer to the world now, no longer an island.

My kids, and my campus students, look to me for answers. None of us knows what the future will hold. Live each day intentionally—you may never see this person again, even your spouse, your kids, your father. Value what you do have—treasure and foster your relationships, especially your family; remember what 3,000 families have lost forever. Finally, take a second look at your life—don't put off seeking answers to the big questions.

I love my kids, and I know I can't keep them from danger as they grow and travel. But what I can give them are my love, my prayers, and the answers I've found, and hope they find their answers along the way.

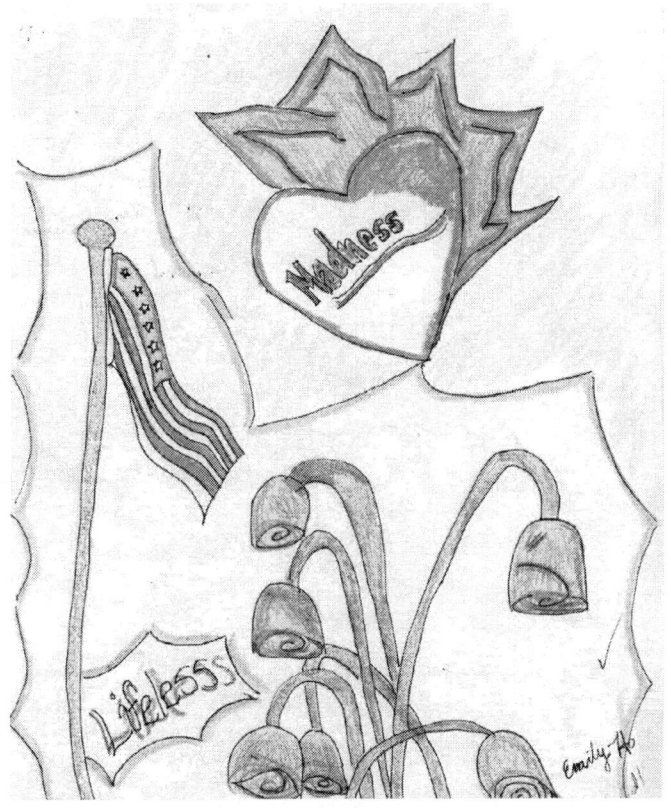

Drawing By: Emily Ho, Bayview Elementary School, Richmond Hill, Ontario.

Chapter 6

The Children Muse

Thoughts from Some of Canada's Children

Poetry submissions were received from grade school students from across Canada. This selection of these heart touching offerings both in this chapter and found throughout the book are representative of the youth of our Nation. Their thoughts are as the thoughts of the adults we interviewed – they are just a little more direct!

I I

I just turned I I
4 days after September I I[th]
Why I I?
Because it is a powerful number,
Every time we hear, see, talk
About September I I[th],
That day will always be in our
HEARTS!

Kahile Gondo, Grade 6

The Tragedy

The day the Twin Towers fell to the ground,
I was the saddest person around
I thought that something like that could never be,
But why, oh why had this happened to me?
Many had lost their parents and their friends
Some mothers even gave birth with no father holding their
hands
Two buildings, two planes, two things in mind,
Fire fighters helping to try and save lives.
Everywhere people were watching and crying
At the thought of so many people dying.
September 11th was a horrible day,
Now all we can do is watch and pray.

Maryam Cissé, Grade 6

9 – 11

September 11th changed us all, in many
different ways.
Physically and emotionally,
The firemen who risked
their lives,
Will never be forgotten.
The people who survived will
never forget the movement
When the planes crashed
through
The Twin Towers.
Everybody who watched
others drop from the
windows will never forget

that moment, when their
lives were taken.
It will never be forgotten.
And I will never forget.
                    Lyla Bussières, Grade 6

Let's Be Safe

Two planes crashed into two buildings.
Twenty-six Canadians were killed.
In that crash thousands of people died.
I want the other people to be saved that go on planes.
                    Canadace Kayseas, Grade 5

The Towers

Though you stood up so high
I heard you nearly touched the sky
I think about it every day
I wish everything would go away
But if this day had never come
I wouldn't have thought about everyone
Although I often wonder why
Now people are happy up in the sky
Let's make the world a better place
For the whole human race
Now everyone's in a blur
I wish we could go back to how things were.
                    Demi Bodnaryk, Grade 5

Freedom

Free, peaceful
Play, run, walk
Family, fun, hurt, weapons
Shooting, dying, hitting
Awful, bad
War

Matthew Currie, Grade 5

War

awful, terrible
shooting, killing, hurting
guns, weapons, love freedom
loving, caring, helping
wonderful, calm
peace

Meagan Knash, Grade 5

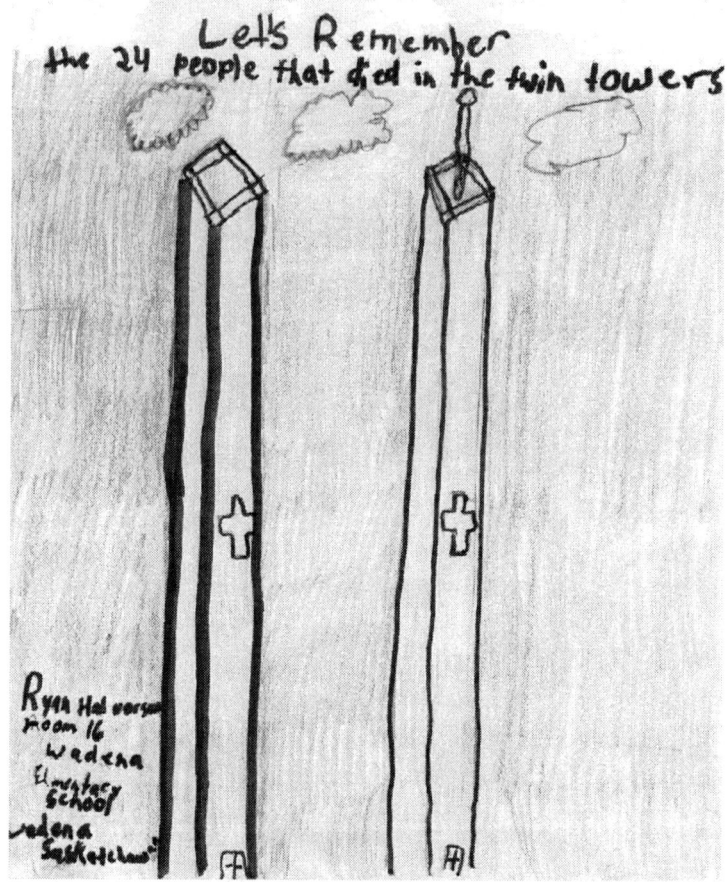

Drawing By: Ryan Halverson, Wadena Elementary School,
Wadena, Saskatchewan

Chapter 7

The Right Thing To Do

Bud Purves: A Tower Executive

Bud Purves is the President of the CN Tower, "Canada's Wonder of the World." He is responsible for overseeing the tower's operation, balancing its entertainment aspect with security. Bud is also a pilot, keeping a plane nearby the CN Tower.

Thirty-five per cent of non-North American visitors to Toronto come to the CN Tower, even though it is not advertised outside North America. That is the nature of the world's tallest structure, visible from every community in the metro area: people are just drawn to it.

That was certainly the case on September 11th, when media "live eye" vans complete with satellite dishes and crews were drawn in droves to the CN Tower as they started to comprehend the magnitude of that morning's attacks in the U.S.

It so happened that morning that we were preparing for the arrival of a dignitary later that week, so both RCMP and Tower staff were already going through security precautions at the building. We were advised of an incident in New York City, so moved in front of our large system of monitors to learn what was happening.

At first, we all thought it was an accident. Even as we watched the second plane hitting the tower live, we thought it must be a replay of the first. Then it was announced that both towers had now been hit, by different planes. As a pilot, I looked at the clear blue sky and the two burning towers, and now knew this was no accident. The RCMP security staff acted as surprised as all of us: this incident had not been anticipated.

Moving to incident status, we immediately turned our thoughts to what we should do, beginning with the perceived level of threat against the CN Tower.

On the one hand, the same thing wouldn't really happen here: this is a concrete tower, not a steel frame office building full of people, furniture and equipment. So we weren't as worried about a specific threat.

On the other hand, the two tallest structures in the downtown area of the U.S.' major city had been attacked. People's minds would naturally turn to buildings like the Sears Tower in Chicago and the CN Tower in Toronto. When you're running the world's tallest structure, it's a logical leap that it could be a target, too. And here we were, running an entertainment centre, with meals, photos, elevator rides, with visitors so far oblivious to the major catastrophe unfolding in New York. We felt incredible sympathy towards the people in the U.S.

We quietly stopped letting new visitors in, and let those who were already inside leave in an orderly fashion. It was the right thing to do.

Tower security and the RCMP did what they needed to do. They secured a perimeter, brought in extra security staff and added higher levels of security checks. As the building emptied, we shut down the tower, and police dogs did a sweep. We spent the rest of the day living through the horror of what was happening to our world.

There were many media interviews, especially on that first day. The media was trying to grapple with understanding the situation, and how it might affect us in Canada. Media anchors like Lloyd Robertson of CTV and Anne Romer of talk radio were gauging our reaction in order to guide Canadians on the right response. Anne wanted to know what we were going to do at the CN Tower; was it going to shut down to visitors?

It was our next tough decision, how to respond on the day after. The easiest thing to do, I told her, is to shut things down, to turn our community into an armed camp. But that's not necessarily the right thing to do. It is our responsibility to balance risks with expectations, and this responsibility was something that I took in a strongly personal way on September 11th. I am an optimist: once each of us takes responsible action, it will work out.

So we decided to open up on September 12th. At 9 a.m., I stood at the front door to see if anyone would show up. Four thousand people did! We ended up having one of our strongest weeks, due in no small measure to the many visitors stranded in Toronto by the attacks. But I like to think that there is a little optimist in each of us, and people weren't going to let the attacks stop them from going up into towers. I was proud of our decision, of our heightened security staff, and most of all, of our visitors.

The Tower faced longer term decisions about what to do: should we curtail activities? Should we close down to visitors? How should we balance the legitimate objectives of security and entertainment? We met with people from other towers—the Empire State Building, the Sears Tower, the London Eye—to share learnings.

One thing seemed certain: things had changed permanently. Gone was the culture of the mid-90's, what some call the "experience" economy, where in the retail and entertainment business, "everything's a show." Society was a little harder now, more tolerant of rules in place, including line-ups, searches and inconveniences. Longer lines and more costly service were being accepted as part of the new reality.

Some good has come out of September 11th. For one thing, it caused us to think hard about what the real value of the CN Tower is to customers. Lots of customers began to call us right after September 11th, and the calls keep coming still. We listen to their expectations and concerns, and err on the side of caution. We need to respect the efforts of those who are still travelling. As a result, we are in closer contact with our customers now, and have a better offering than we had before. We hired additional staff to engage and entertain our visitors at every step of their CN Tower experience, even in the inevitable line-ups at the entrances.

Security has tightened, of course. Indeed there has been a profound change. We've spent over a million dollars in hardware, baggage screening and other sophisticated detection devices, dogs and equipment to "sniff" suspicious packages, changes to elevators, more security staff, drills. The liaison with the RCMP and CSIS has ramped up a level: both now know our building a lot better. We've curtailed some activities, but most are going ahead, including events for dignitaries at the Tower.

Business did drop off after the first week, but started to recover in a couple of months and is strengthening monthly. People who have come back often remark that there is so much more to see and do at the CN Tower than just a tall tower. We've taken some promotional steps: we unveiled "Come and See Canada's Wonder of the World" and have been in close touch with concierges at hotels in town, finding out who'll be staying in town and offering discounts to visitors.

We have a responsibility to do the right thing in this new reality. We need to be able to look our children in the eyes and assure them that the world can be a safe place, but that we need to take care of each other: each of us has a responsibility, and we need to take it seriously. We should appreciate what we have in Canada, and take a new look at familiar things. The CN Tower is just an example of that: it stands as an example of us taking responsibility, profoundly re-thinking the right security / entertainment mix and restoring the confidence of the public. It's the right thing to do.

Drawing by: Nika Shakita, Age 13, Bayview Hill E. S., Richmond Hill, Ontario

Chapter 8

Good Prevailed

Caroline Danis: A Student

Caroline Danis has a degree in journalism and is from Gatineau, Quebec. She also works in our Nation's capital in the Parliament buildings. Representing the next generation of leaders and communicators in this country, Caroline's story of moving from disbelief to fear to hope is bound to inspire you!

The thing I remember most about September 11th is the bodies falling from the sky. To think that people would be so desperate they would rather jump to their death than face the flames. No one should have to make that choice. Ten years from now perhaps something different will stand out – like where I was when I found out ...

In my mind and heart is burned an image of a classroom full of students transfixed in disbelief and sadness.

September 11th began as any other day. In my second year of journalism studies at Cité Collegiale in Ottawa, it was a beautiful fall day. Unexpectedly and with solemn looks, a professor entered our classroom and turned on the television set. Immediately our curiosity was piqued. What could be such a big deal to cause this disruption? It did not take long for us to find out. We joined the rest of the world shortly after the south tower fell.

At first I did not think anything. Really. I could think of nothing. It was too incredible. Too unbelievable to be true. This could not be happening. Why would someone do this? In time my mind moved to my family, my boyfriend, his family. Where are they? Could any of them be in danger? I made a mental checklist. All of my loved ones must be safe. Then, back to unbelief. Surely this was not real. This could not have happened.

My classmates reacted in a variety of ways. Some, like me, were holding back tears — not wanting the others to see any sign of weakness. We were budding journalists, after all. Others moved from nervous laughter to quiet reflection. Though we all wanted people to be quiet, so that we could hear the news, we could not seem to stop talking. Back to disbelief.

Then it struck me — what will be next? Will the other tower fall? Will there be more planes? What is happening at the Pentagon? I need to leave here. Home. I needed to call home. Did they know? What about my boyfriend? Did he know? His parents? Oh no! They had flown somewhere in the United States the night before. Where were they? New York perhaps? Washington? They could be anywhere!

Time seemed to stand still as I made my way to make the calls. I reached my mother first. For the moment she remained in blissful ignorance of the horror the rest of the world was experiencing. I listened as she turned on the television and moved through the range of emotions so many others knew too well.

Leaving her to take it in, the next call was to Josh. He was very upset and unable to remain at work. The main focus of his thoughts was for his parents, now grounded in Chicago — thank God it wasn't New York. But were they alright? The United States suddenly seemed so small. Chicago seemed as New York. He had to reach them and hear their voices.

After minutes that seemed as hours, everyone had been accounted for. My thoughts now turned to my part time job. I was scheduled to work that afternoon at the gift shop, in downtown Ottawa, in the Centre Block of Canada's Parliament buildings. Should I go in? Would we be open? My father was frantic I would even consider going. Still, I could not really think — it still seemed so unreal — why wouldn't I go to work?

Reality began to sink in as I arrived downtown. Why were the streets closed off? A bomb threat, someone said. I tried to find a safe route but the only choices I had were to pass the US Embassy, the Parliament Buildings or the Department of National Defence. The deeper in reality set, the more fearful and frantic I became. The police, the people, the stress of it all! I needed to go home.

Like most of the world the rest of the day was spent in front of the television contemplating why. What could possibly motivate such hatred?

After the attacks it seemed I should do something to help, but what? What could I do? I had no money to send — starving student and all! New York was too far away and they had lots of help already. So, I did the two things I could do. I gave blood and I prayed. These were all I knew to do yet in retrospect I think these were two of the most important gifts that could be given.

It was hard to go back to work. No one wanted to be there. Security was so tight now it only served to reinforce the fear. The gift shop had stayed closed to the public for a week. Normally a loyal and compliant employee I refused to work in the basement stock room. The thought of being trapped under tons of rubble terrified me. Just a week earlier the thought had never crossed my mind.

Fear of an attack on the building wasn't the only thing either. By now it was anthrax. Just a few days earlier I had never even heard of anthrax. Now I was afraid to open the mail and parcels at work for fear of death. So much had changed in a few short days.

I was changed. All of a sudden it was difficult to trust people. Fear of buildings falling, fear of opening mail and now fear of people. Touching things others had touched now bothered me. Planes flying overhead – especially near the Parliament buildings – the fighter jets protecting this no-fly zone - caused my heart to race.

Someone told me once that God could turn bad things into good things. Could that be true? It began to occur to me that not all of the changes were so negative. This surprised me. I had gained a new-found respect for law enforcement, emergency service workers, firemen, and all those who helped. They so impressed me. In spite of the odds, hard work and the very horror of the situation, they pressed on, even when there seemed to be no end in sight. They continued in hope.

And then, there were those people who in spite of the tragedy did so many good deeds. For example, there was one man in New York who opened his restaurant for the workers. You wouldn't normally see someone whose livelihood had just been traumatically interrupted keep pushing forward and feeding people for free!

Over the days following the terrorist attack I saw the good in people emerge, not just in spite of the horror but as a result of it! If the people in New York and Washington could respond with hope, and be changed for good in the midst of disaster, so too could I.

Since September 11th I have changed in recognizable ways. I think there are also ways that I have changed that I don't even understand, nor may not for many years to come. Everyone has. We can't help but be changed by this. We all thought that North Americans were untouchable but now we know that no one is. That knowledge can't help but change us all.

Even though we have lost our innocence, that loss has left us with a certain wisdom. A wisdom that has changed my perception of life and people. A wisdom that teaches us we can learn something out of every situation. In fact, it is through the most drastic events of our lifetime that we can learn the most important lessons.

Osama Bin Laden taught me a number of life lessons. He meant them for evil but God has used them for good in my life. My determination is to take those life lessons and teach them to my children. They will learn how to resolve conflict without violence, that retaliation is not the answer and that we must look for the commonalities we share with our neighbours – not focus on our differences and allow them to divide us.

I will teach them not to think of themselves as better than others, never to take life for granted – for it can all change in an instant - to understand that you cannot solve everyone's problems, and not to allow hate to empower their lives.

Above all, I will teach my children that good prevailed on September 11th 2001.

Drawing By: Kimberley Ngan, Age 13, Bayview Hill E. S., Richmond Hill, Ontario

Chapter 9

The Main Thing

Gordon MacLeod: A Minister

Reverend Gordon MacLeod is a Minister at Lewisville Baptist Church in Moncton, New Brunswick. As flights were diverted to many locations on the Canadian east coast, Moncton included, churches from every denomination rose to the occasion. They took complete strangers into their homes for meals, lodging and some much needed TLC. Hear how one such church responded and how this minister taught his congregation about true security.

It was shortly after the second tower was struck we heard the news. By this time much of the world knew this was more than an accident – it was an attack. My staff and I were in the middle of our weekly meeting when we were told. Initially our conclusion was this must be a mistake, some kind of hoax. It was just too awful to be true. We began to search for the truth.

Swinging around in my chair, fingers quickly typed www.cnn.com across the keyboard. Nothing. The server was completely overloaded. We tried other network websites. They too were overloaded. Someone plugged in the old television that sat in the corner of my office. To our dismay, lacking a cable connection, we could raise no signal.

It was at this point we assumed the report was true. First we cried. Then we began to pray. Then came time for action.

The first call was to my wife. Busy at work, she did not know of the drama unfolding. I was glad to be the one to tell her. Next came phone calls to my friends in the United States. Somehow I just felt I needed to call them, to hear their voices, and tell them we were praying. To this day I make a conscious effort to keep in touch with them much more so than before.

As a minister, once I had spoken with my own family my focus turned to the spiritual family in my care, and to how as a church family we could be of service. We did not have to look very far. Dozens of planes were being diverted to the Moncton airport. Authorities were taking stranded passengers to the Moncton Coliseum as a starting point. From there housing and meals were arranged. This is where my congregation started. I was so proud of them. Without even having time to organize our response they had jumped in with both feet to serve. Several of our parishioners went to the Coliseum where they offered and gave help and hospitality to these unexpected guests, opening up their homes and their cupboards.

As the congregation went to work addressing the physical needs of those around them, my attention needed to quickly turn to addressing their spiritual needs – for surely there would be many.

Not surprisingly my focus was driven back to the ultimate questions of life – first and foremost, including a refocusing on my own relationship with God. After all, Ministers are people too! Before I could offer the depth of comfort that would be required of me, I needed to seek and find comfort for myself. Just like everyone else, I experienced a wide range of emotions. From disbelief and shock, through intense anger and deep sadness, and everything in between.

In my own soul searching and questioning, I was caused to rethink security. Where does it really come from? As North Americans I had not thought we would need to be concerned with personal security. Now I realize we had all felt too secure. Secure in the wrong things really. For we will never find true safety and security through the efforts of man. On a basic level, the security measures we throw up as human beings are still subject to efforts of human beings. There is no guarantee in personal security. Security is a far bigger issue.

I found myself driven to scripture. One passage that struck me particularly was Psalm 33: 16-18:

"The king is not saved by a mighty army; A warrior is not delivered by great strength. A horse is a false hope for victory; Nor does it deliver anyone by its great strength. Behold, the eye of the Lord is on those who fear Him, on those who hope for His loving kindness."[1]

That day, I found comfort in knowing where my true security lay and it was with this I set about to comfort others.

As a minister I have to deal with grief all the time both professionally and personally – so one gets used to it – but now profound sadness permeated. The need for symbolism and ceremony to move through the sadness was stark.

That Sunday we structured our service much like a funeral. Using images, prayers, and language customary to a funeral service was helpful. They caused all of us to grieve appropriately, recognizing we were not alone in our grief, and bringing our focus onto solutions for the grief and pain we all felt. We were moved to look for the hope of eternal life and the promises and security found in God.

Coming together in a spiritual community helped us to then move forward as we served our guests from around the globe, and in coming alongside the rest of the Moncton community as it dealt with and responded to the fallout of terrorism. Our church helped the city put together a book of condolences that was sent to ground zero. New York City, America and the

---

[1] New American Standard Bible Version

world needed one big symbolic funeral service. We had been helped by our service and we wanted to play our part in the world's grief.

Our church is not the same since September 11th. So much good has come through the bad – for often times absolutely amazing and wonderful things come out of the truly awful things in life.

We saw triumph through sacrifice, incredible connections between people and heard stories about the positive results in the lives of people. People were significantly touched and permanently changed for the good.

We saw what happens when ordinary people do extraordinary things in an extraordinary situation. People from every walk of life in New York, Moncton and in many corners of the world, touching and being touched by the events and each other. We saw and heard those extraordinary stories involving ordinary people – from dramatic rescues, to sacrifice of life for another, to "serving a cup of cold water in Jesus' name".

The ordinary has changed forever. We have learned that the extraordinary is all around us. I believe it is there because it reflects God. We just don't look for it often enough.

Our focus has changed too. The focus of people, in our church, our community and around the world was driven back to the ultimate questions of life. And to me, as a minister of God, it is especially heartening to watch as people see and find the answers to those questions in relationship with God. People are asking, "How does a relationship with God affect me?" "What am I really about?" "Does my life really reflect that?" "Does my focus reflect how I feel about God and others, and how He feels about me?"

People are changing as a result of the answers they are finding to these questions. I am no exception.

After the 11th and now, I spend a lot of time with young people. It began shortly after the attacks with a 15 year old boy. He wanted me to tell him what life is all about. The next generation has been affected deeply by this and we must come alongside them and teach them about faith and hope and love – teach them about God and how to know Him.

Too, I focus more energy on those things that are of the utmost importance – family. The world needs family. Too often we take those we love the most for granted. We act as if we have forever and we don't. All of us have had a stern reminder that anything can happen at any time. So these days I foster a "seize the day" mentality.

Another important change in my own life has been to rethink and count the cost of things. Like Todd Beamer and those of flight 93, it is more important than ever to be willing to lay down our lives for what is good and right and true – regardless of cost to ourselves. I am going to Serbia, Bosnia and Croatia this year for a short term project to teach and help the churches there. If this could happen here then it could happen there. I must be willing to invest my life when called to.

September 11th pushed me to think about things that I have not thought about for a long time. Personally I have been renewed. I was moved to think back to the basics of my faith. What I believe in and why. Through that my faith is deeper, wider and stronger as is my personal journey with God. My professional one has sharpened and focused.

I am determined to take a look at what the "main things" in life are and remain focused on them - God, family, others and life in service to them. That too is my desire for the next generation as together we attempt to find a positive legacy to the tragedy of September's terrorism. My hope is that they too will learn and understand what are the "main things" and they will always remember that the "main thing" must remain the "main thing"!

My climbing tree makes me feel safe and secure. I hope that you have a special place like my climbing tree.

Abbey ♡
Age 7.

Drawing by: Abbey, Age 7, Banded Peak School, Bragg Creek, Alberta

Chapter 10

Parallel Lives

Roger Clarkson: A Friend

Roger Clarkson is an executive with SpencerStuart, a global search firm, in Toronto. His best friend since childhood was one of the Canadians who lost his life in New York. Roger candidly and openly talks about his friend and the deep loss he has had to come to grips with, how he understands that it could have been any of us, and his own sense of responsibility as a survivor to leave a legacy in the wake of 9/11.

On the Sunday evening following September 11th, the phone rang and my wife answered it. As soon as she repeated one word, "Donald", I just knew the call was about Donald Robson, and that he had been killed at the World Trade Center.

Donald and I grew up together. His parents owned the farm next to ours, and we spent a lot of time together in our pre-teen and teenage years especially.

Several years ago, he moved to the U.S. to pursue his career. He was working at the World Trade Center in 1993 when the first terrorist attack happened. He went back to work the next day, and reported to work once more on September 11th, at Cantor Fitzgerald on the 103rd floor of the World Trade Center.

That morning began routinely for me as well. I was in the office, participating in our regular weekly Tuesday morning meeting. It wound up about five minutes to nine, and as we came out, my assistant Chris told me of the announcement, that a plane had gone into the World Trade Center.

Ten minutes later, I came out of my office to hear that a second plane had gone in. I knew something unique and scary was going on.

Then the Pentagon attack. Here was something our generation hadn't dealt with before.

My first thoughts turned to my family. Are they aware of what's going on? Are they safe? Are there any potential threats to Canada? I called my wife, then my daughter in Toronto, thankfully getting through to both right away. It took a little longer to reach my second daughter in Halifax. An hour, only, yet one of the longest hours of my life, but we did get through and she was all right.

Our thoughts turned to our own situation. Spencer Stuart is located in a downtown Toronto highrise, literally one block from the major towers. There was as yet no official word, but word-of-mouth spread that the towers were evacuating and people were pouring onto the streets.

We held an impromptu meeting deliberating what to do at our office. Some said we needed to carry on, not to overreact. This was an attack on the U.S., and Canada was not likely at risk. Others pointed out the major nature of this event, how the tragedy immediately affected us all, and that in no way could we assess the real risk without more information. An incident that was geographically distant became much closer.

The second view bore out. We did decide to close the office. Whatever the real risk, people felt better being able to go home to their families. And no work was getting done anyway, by any of us: the only calls coming in or going out were with loved ones.

There were lots of e-mails, though. Spencer Stuart is a global company, and partners from around the world were seeking information about the attacks, commenting on the terrible tragedy, and voicing their strong support and heartfelt thoughts for our colleagues in New York. Our offices there are located in the downtown Manhattan area, and we desperately sought word from them. E-mails began to arrive, cryptic but reassuring. The New York office was safe, our colleagues were all right. Communications for the whole downtown had been lost, and the office was shut down, but no one was hurt. An incident that was happening to strangers became one that was happening to friends.

Our family gathered around the TV, the same way and with the same emotional and physical response as when John Kennedy was shot. Donald and I were in Grade 13, I can still recall the teacher coming in to the classroom in tears, unable to say or do anything but send the class home.

There was more tension leading up to that—the Cold War, domestic tensions—we lived in a time of heightened awareness then. This time the impact was much worse—North America and the western world had been relaxed, on a ten year high, our collective guard let down.

My wife and daughter and I looked at each other. My daughter studied psychology at Queen's, and my other daughter is studying political science at Dalhousie, so we entered into a lot of discussion and reflection. Shock, disbelief, uncertainty: these were our feelings. It was suddenly important for us to be in touch with one another, and we were very glad that we could be. An incident that was impersonal became one that was personal.

This was the first time the North American continent had been attacked from the outside, and this attack was not just anywhere, but in the heart of our major city. The naked boldness of the attack unmasked the extent of the threat we now faced from organized terrorism. The U.S. consulate is just up the block from my office downtown Toronto, and I was jarred to see major demonstrations and police barricades on my return to work later that week. Seeing the demonstrators on one side, the police on the other, the metal barricade between, illustrated the divide we were now so keenly aware of, and the ongoing conflict that was far from over, perhaps only just beginning. An incident that was a New York problem became a U.S. problem, and a U.S. problem became a North American one.

And then that weekend, the call came. A close friend had been killed. Someone I grew up with, someone whose school and play and work paralleled my own and so many others. Someone with a beautiful wife, two young sons, a wonderful smile, a twinkle in his eye: a joy to be with. An incident that had been nasty became intensely personal.

Talk turned to funeral arrangements. There was to be one in Connecticut and a second here in Toronto. But the family couldn't confirm the Toronto date. Don's wife had five more services that she knew of, for very close friends, all lost at the World Trade Center.

I was able to spend some time with Donald's sister Nancy and their family after the funeral was finally held. Donald's wife had been staying with them and was leaving to return home alone. A very trying time.

I wrote to Don's wife after that, and got a charming letter back. I hadn't really expected or sought any response, I just wanted her to know our thoughts and prayers, but she showed me how strong her character is and it gave me a much needed lift, reassurance in what humans can do when faced with tremendous challenges.

It was a clarion call to me. I survived September 11th, we survived September 11th, and we are called on to respond. An incident that was an action against us became one where we need to act.

We simplified our lives, postponing expenditures, limiting work travel, spending more time with family and friends. And appreciating that time, and what we do have.

More than appreciation, we have a new awareness of our responsibilities, to protect what we do have. North America's isolation ended on September 11th, along with so much else. We know we can't relax too much; we have to be prepared to defend and protect our country. A strong defence costs money, and requires leadership with courage and clarity.

I ask questions now that I might have skimmed over before. How much of this is driven by the gap between rich and poor? Between Islam and Christianity? Between Israel and Palestine? This isn't at its heart about these things, although there are economic, religious and factional overtones. This is about communication, but only to a point. Suicide bombers flying planes full of innocent people into buildings full of innocent people: how do you fight against that?

This is about evil and hatred. These are terrorists, and these terrorists are neither poor nor of Islam. These are humans, but humans with completely different moral standards. This is about fighting age-old battles, endless battles, with new weapons. For every death, another death, it will never stop unless someone stops it. A friend of mine said "If you really want it to stop, take the men out of the room, and put in the mothers."

This generation is better traveled and better informed of other cultures than any before it, but had not experienced war. Other generations each experienced war: World War I, World War II, Korea, Vietnam. Now, these mushroom clouds of dust as people ran frantically from collapsing buildings ushers in this generation's experience of war.

Terrorism's real threat is its ability to destabilize. One more attack could have destabilized our economy and our society.

President Bush in particular showed strong leadership in getting out ahead of this, in encouraging spending and both the U.S. and Canada are now much stronger than we would have been as a result. An incident that was meant to weaken and isolate us has made us stronger and more united.

The Mayor of New York, too, demonstrated great leadership and acted as an able and confident spokesperson. "I love New York" isn't just a slogan with a symbol of a heart any more, but a real inspiration to us all, reminding us of the spirit of Americans in general and New Yorkers specifically.

Two months after September 11th, my wife Susan and I flew down to Halifax to spend some time with our daughter there. On the Monday morning, an American Airlines Airbus crashed into Queen's, New York. No one knew what happened, or if it was the beginning of a new round of attacks.

On Tuesday, we looked out at our own Airbus, the same plane, being readied to fly us home. We had no hesitation, we had faith. We got back on.

We can't let these events—and the fear they stoke—paralyze us. We survived September 11th and we have to keep on living. Yes, we are aware of our fears, but we can't let them conquer us. Those who died on September 11th would have expected us to get on with our lives. I think of the Queen Mother and her husband walking among the people during the London blitz, after Buckingham Palace had been bombed. That's what endeared her to the people. Each of us have our own actions to take and we can and will make a difference. An incident intended to terrify us has given us hope.

This summer, up at the cottage, we are going to plant a tree in memory of Donald. It will help us to remember him and all the good times we shared before September 11th.

Drawing By: Joyce Wong, 13 years old, Bayview Hill E. S., Richmond Hill, Ontario

Chapter 11

Helplessness

Dr. Arlette Lefebvre: A Doctor

Dr. Arlette Lefebvre is a Child Psychiatrist on staff at The Hospital for Sick Children in Toronto, and Associate Professor of Psychiatry at the University of Toronto (Faculty of Medicine), her medical school "alma mater". Affectionately known to her patients and their families as "Dr.Froggie", Arlette was the architect of the HSC Humour Library, founder of the first Canadian fund for children with AIDS and is actively involved in a broad range of community activities. In 1999, Dr. Lefebvre co-authored the book "Taking Your Kids On-line: How and When to Introduce Children to the Internet", and became a member of the Order of Canada.

It is difficult not to feel helpless in the face of overwhelming traumatic events. I think we all sat there feeling completely helpless as we watched events unfold in New York and Washington on September 11th. Thousands of trapped office workers, hundreds of emergency workers, victims of horrendous violence, and almost all of us were intimately connected to them by live television.

We doctors are no exception. Our whole being is wrapped up in needing to help people, to alleviate suffering and to enhance quality of life. Within minutes of the attacks on September 11th, medical staff rushed to area hospitals prepared to treat the injured. Hundreds of thousands of us across the continent rushed to the Red Cross to donate blood for the victims. Ambulances lined up for blocks around the World Trade Center waiting for the dust to settle and the wounded to be evacuated.

The dust did settle, although it took days and even weeks, but the wounded never did come out. The harsh reality was that you either walked away or you were killed that day. Emergency rooms stood empty. Doctors and nurses felt helpless. Ambulance crews eventually returned to their own homes and children.

Parents felt helpless that day, too, as they watched and listened to their children. Sometimes we assume that because children are such frequent watchers of TV and users of the Internet that they completely understand what they are seeing and using. Don't assume kids of any age understand the words they are hearing and repeating. Of course children are people too, and just as susceptible to life's deceptions and temptations as the rest of us.

We'd already invested a lot of energy in research of, and preparation for, traumatic stress before that horrible day. We knew that children who watched TV coverage of the Oklahoma City bombing exhibited markedly more Post Traumatic Stress Disorder (PTSD) symptoms seven weeks after the bombing than children who did not. This was true for children who had not been directly affected by the bombing as well as for those who had lost a family member. The Gulf War had equally traumatic effects: two-thirds of Kuwaiti children reported viewing TV images of violence and death, the type of exposure associated with increases in PTSD symptoms. Clearly, with the sheer scale and exposure of September 11th, many more children would be left with PTSD symptoms in its wake.

Broadcasting of disasters and traumatic events are by no means the only triggers of stress and anxiety in children. My heart breaks every time I think of the popularity of violent children's programming, led by professional wrestling spectacles, and of violent children's video games and internet sites. I'm concerned that one of our kids' favourite sites is neopets.com, where young children are taught how to gamble, by earning and then wagering points on "games". ICQ and on-line casino gambling are so closely connected that our kids can't go on-line to chat without being exposed to hard-sell gambling sites. Don't get me wrong, I'm not crusading against children being on-line or watching TV—I've spent many years trying to help both children and parents understand the right ways and times to use these powerful tools—we need not feel helpless in this.

Children don't all react the same way to media coverage of disasters like September 11th. A number of factors influence how they will react. It depends on their age, developmental level and temperament, and the amount of media exposure. They will be much more susceptible if they know someone who died or themselves have been a victim of violence or trauma in the past. They will take cues from what they sense from their parents, teachers and other adults around them: anxiety, tension, fear, anger, nonchalance.

But a lot of children were traumatized by the media coverage of September 11th. Seeing those planes full of people flying into those buildings full of people, seeing the tremendous explosions and fires, the buildings crumbling and the clouds of choking dust, and seeing these things over and over again, cannot help but affect someone deeply (and not just children, either.)

We talked to a lot of children who feared dust falling, on their toys, beds, homes. We encouraged children to draw pictures, and saw many draw their own school or another familiar building blowing up. We met many children who experienced nightmares for many weeks after the experience.

Children reacted with both realistic and unrealistic fears. And for every child with visible anxieties, there are others who thought the whole thing was cool, like a video game. And still others, especially the very young, who didn't give it much thought at all, not grasping the reality or significance of the images, or connecting them with attacks and deaths. Don't be surprised if your child doesn't see the events that occurred as real or upsetting.

Generally, children reacted to September 11th in three ways:

- *fear:* becoming more fearful of the world around them: "Bad World Syndrome",

- *anger:* becoming more aggressive and mean (and/or)

- *desensitized:* becoming less sensitive to the suffering of others: "getting used to it."

There are steps that parents can take to feel less helpless in the face of these reactions. I like to think of them as the "3 M's" of helping children handle disaster-related anxiety: <u>monitor, mediate and mitigate.</u>

Monitoring is especially important with young children. It involves carefully screening what they are watching, and never leaving the TV on when unattended. Parents themselves should limit the amount of CNN they allow themselves to watch every day. Use other media to stay up-to-date (e.g. CNN on-line, radio in the car, newspapers.)

Mediating begins by spending time and listening to children's concerns. This is perhaps the most significant thing parents and physicians can do to help. Here are some things to listen and watch for[2]:

---

[2] These symptoms and observations are summarized by Dr. Lefebvre in a PowerPoint presentation at media-awareness.ca

	In Preschoolers	Middle Childhood	Adolescents
Signs of stress	► thumb-sucking ► bed-wetting ► fear of the dark ► clinging to parents	► irritability ► whining ► nightmares ► sibling rivalry	► preoccupation with CNN and news ► insomnia, irritability ► rebelliousness at home ► social withdrawal
Watch for	► uncontrollable crying ► loss of appetite ► sleep disruption	► decreased school performance ► school refusal	► substance abuse ► depression ► school absenteeism

If you note some of these signs, ask children about their concerns: listen first. Then you can begin to explain what they have already seen or heard about the attacks, but not more: parents often go overboard with long, detailed explanations about politics or religion beyond the child's specific concern. Make a distinction between traditional wars between countries and the acts of terrorist minorities; discourage generalizations! Above all, be honest in answering their questions.

Mitigating runs the gamut from reassuring young children that they are safe, to reminding adolescents of new safety measures being taken to ensure their safety. Keep family routines structured and predictable and keep kids busy with normal stuff. Focus on extraordinary acts of kindness which tragedies bring out in people. Parents can help by being a good role model: carry on with life!

So there are things that parents, physicians, educators and children themselves can do to help in times of disaster and related media coverage. We need not feel completely helpless.

However, I also caution adults who feel that they must prepare children for the worst that could possibly happen. There are things in life beyond our control, of our ability to predict or prevent. There is a place in life for some stress and tension, but not for constant anxiety and fear. There is a time in life when we can and must help, and there are times in life when we must sit helplessly by.

September 11th was one of those times, but it too passes. I'm reminded of the words of Mahatma Gandhi:

"When I despair, I remember that all through history the ways of truth and love have always won. There have been tyrants, and murderers, and for a time they can even seem invincible, but in the end they always fail. Think of it . . . Always."

"I wonder if they will ever find Bin Laden?
I wonder if Bin Laden will go to heaven?
I wonder what the people on the plane felt?
I wonder if the firefighters felt worried going into the buildings?
I wonder if the rescue workers thought they would ever see their family again?
I wonder how people in the military felt going into Afghanistan?
I wonder if there ever will be another event like this that will scare me to the core?"

Poem and Drawing by: Taylor Gidosh, Grade 4, Warburg School, Warburg Alberta

Chapter 12

A Blessed Nation

Professor Mohamed Bayoumi: A Muslim

Mohamed Bayoumi is Professor Emeritus at Queen's University, Kingston, Ontario.   While retired from full-time teaching, Professor Bayoumi stays active by teaching courses at Queen's and the Royal Military College, by serving as Vice-Chair of Patient Care and Quality Control on the board of the Kingston General Hospital ("KGH"), and serving in leadership at Kingston's Islamic Centre.

Two things are etched forever in my memory about September 11th.

Etched in my mind is the image of an airplane going through a building. I cannot get it out of my head. Even now, I see it vividly almost all the time.

Etched in my heart is the outpouring of kindness with which I have been showered by people. Both people known to me and people not known to me at all. This is the legacy of September 11th.

A few minutes before 9:00 a.m. on September 11th, I headed into a meeting with the board Chair, Vice-Chair and two staff members on patient care at KGH. For almost two hours we talked about the importance of quality care, of service excellence, of understanding and meeting patients' needs, oblivious of what was going on outside the room. Strangely set apart from the rest of the world, we were privileged to be able to focus on what knit us together: allocating the resources at our disposal, ensuring care, recovery and healing.

And so it was in my car on the way home that I first heard the news. CBC radio is always on in the car, and they had continuous coverage from the scenes in New York and Washington.

I couldn't imagine something like that happening. It was still a confused picture then, at 11:00 a.m. It was hard to believe that airplanes would be directed into office buildings full of people.

Our first thoughts turned to the immediate members of our family. My wife and I have three children: those in Kingston and Toronto both got in touch with us right away, but neither of us were able to reach our son in New York City.

Our son teaches at Brooklyn College but lives in Manhattan, not far from the World Trade Center. We found out he wasn't on campus that day, but was working at home.

We used to have an arrangement with all our kids to talk every week on Sunday. Even if it was just for a few minutes, we wanted to be in close touch, you always want that when your son or daughter moves away. But we had got out of that habit lately. It's funny how easy it is to take for granted life's blessings: our university, our hospital, our home, our family.

Finally, after 3:00 p.m., our son was able to get through to us. In retrospect, it was only four or five hours, but it seemed like an eternity, full of anxiety and uncertainty. He was fine. We agreed to call each other every few hours, and spoke daily for a long time after that.

My son and I were following the news very closely for the next few days. We exchanged notes frequently, trying to help one another build a picture of what happened, and why, and what would happen now, and why. Trying to find the truth behind it all.

There is evil in the world; horrific things do happen. Yet humanity has so much more positive to offer, and the way to respond to evil is through living our lives in a positive way. We can choose to let evil negatively affect our lives, to turn us against one another and to accentuate our differences. Or we can acknowledge evil as part of our experience but choose not to let it overwhelm us. We can focus on our lack, or celebrate our blessings.

Since September 11th, my son and I have both been approached by many people, some known to us and others not, some concerned for our safety and others interested in us speaking about our experiences.

The Chair of KGH organized a meeting for the full staff, and asked me to join him. The purpose was to give them our full support, knowing that some had relatives in the U.S., or knew colleagues from Canada working in the U.S., and that some were Muslims or Arabs on staff. Our pastoral care committee, which provides care in the tradition of people's choice, led a further session aimed at meeting spiritual needs. The Queen's Chaplain and Interfaith Council held a special service at Grant Hall in the heart of the campus. Over 1,500 people attended, filling Grant Hall and overflowing to the grounds and streets outside. It was so clear that everyone there needed healing, and this service was a moving event and a step in that journey. I was honoured to be invited to participate. We live in a society often cynical of our leaders, yet in this time of crisis, we realized how blessed we are to have such leadership.

The Islamic Centre, which includes a mosque, decided to hold an open house shortly after September 11th. We had no idea if any one would be interested or if it was a good idea. But on the day itself, over one thousand people came, and listened, and talked. My son and I both have had other opportunities to speak since then: at churches, at schools, at workplaces, to the media.

One call I received stood out among the others. A Vice-President of the University, someone I knew only slightly, called me up in the days following September 11th. He was calling in his capacity as a leader of the local Presbyterian church, to express their concern for me as a visible member of the Muslim community, that I might be subject to persecution or trouble as a result of September 11th.

Yet in the months since, there has been only one incident in Kingston. Between classes at Queen's, one student made derogatory comments to another who appeared to be a Muslim. The University's Principal took decisive and strong action to intervene, and that sent a signal that such incidents wouldn't be tolerated.

We are such a blessed nation in Canada. In the past few years, problems have surfaced in many places around the world: South Africa, Bosnia, Kosovo. In those places, people didn't talk, and the initial problems grew into time bombs that blew up. When people fail to talk with one another, they can never understand one another. They will never recognize their commonalities, instead seeing their differences and accentuating these.

That's what stands out for me about Canada. We experienced a problem on September 11th, and we talked with one another about it. We discussed our problems, exposing our differences, our issues, and our commonalities, rather than stifling them and waiting 'til something else happens. The way to deal with evil is to expose it to the light, not to leave it in the darkness. The way to deal with evil is to celebrate our blessings.

In a strange way, then, I am more optimistic about the future than I was before September 11th. Humanity has gone through many negative—even horrific—experiences, like wars, and it is easy to be held in their grip, to be obsessed by these. But we didn't let ourselves be held in the grip of evil, we learned and used it for good. People communicated to one another, shared their feelings, and started to know one another. We will get through this. We are a nation blessed.

Drawing By: Harley Spencer, Grade 4, Warburg School, Warburg, Alberta

Chapter 13

Comrades

Ben Addley – An Emergency Services Worker

Ben Addley is Operations Manager for Peel Region Ambulance Services where he is responsible for, among other things, staffing, hospital issues and scene control. The Peel Region encompasses Canada's busiest airport, Lester B. Pearson International in Toronto. Ben's story gives us confidence in the men and women whom we count on to be there should such a traumatic event ever happen here in Canada. Within minutes of the planes hitting the Twin Towers a full scale response was well in motion in Peel Region as they prepared for any eventuality.

When the first plane hit, I was at work taking part in paramedic training with eleven others. We had just gone into the crew room for a break when the news broke. At this point only the first strike had taken place so we decided to extend our break a little and watch the news as it unfolded.

As we all discussed what our own response would be if something like that had happened in our jurisdiction, the second plane hit. Our immediate response was one of shock, yet the emergency services training in us turned on and we quickly put all of our staff on notice to stay in and on alert and moved into a management planning meeting. Our first considerations were about our own airport – Lester B. Pearson International in Toronto – and to the implications for our own response.

My wife Marci is a para-medic as well, home on maternity leave at the time, she called me. From the start it struck very close to home for me. One of the first things that crossed my mind was the number of schools and day care centers that would have to face helping children whose parents never returned to pick them up. We chatted briefly – I was thankful that she and I had our vocations in common and she knew full well how I would be feeling and what I had to do. Right now, there was not much time for talking and thinking about anything beyond duty.

Staff were kept on and every extra vehicle was readied. Because we had a lot of the staff in for the training session, we instantly had extra crews and vehicles ready to go. We gathered all the equipment we could get our hands on. We knew that with the scale of the disaster in New York they would need these resources – we could help supply them. By that first evening we had mobilized a third of our own force with a raft of supplies and were ready to go to their aid at a moment's notice.

As we sat and watched the scene continue to unfold on television, we all wanted to go, but we knew it had to be beneficial and we had to deploy our resources where they were best utilized. It was difficult to stay here and wait to see when and where we were needed. And, we had work here to do. There were many planes diverted to Canada - we knew the numbers, the locations they were routed to and when they were arriving. Crews needed to be dispatched to our own airport.

The emergency services group is a tight one – we are all comrades – family really. Whether in Toronto or New York – each of us knows what we all go through in this line of work. The firefighters in New York are para-medics too. From the beginning we felt a part of the attack – these were our people doing the same job we do and would have done had it happened here.

The Senior Operations Manager made contact with the airport. Though we had few facts at this point, we all knew this was a large incident that required a major response. Within two hours of the first plane hitting, the disaster planning committee had been called together at the airport, including all of the regional representatives, and a plan was in place to handle any potential eventuality that could affect our own area.

We planned and worked steadily and quickly – but very somberly. Though we were not directly affected by the attacks in Washington and New York, the event brought momentum to a lot of planning for our own system and disaster response plans. Our initial planning session ran for thirty hours straight. For the first week following the attack our shifts ran for 24 hours a day.

Over the coming days, each of our four platoons traveled to Ground Zero on their days off, to pay their respects. I had the privilege of playing the role of honour guard during the removal of a number of bodies. This experience of camaraderie is one that will never leave me. As EMS workers we were already comrades, but now even more so.

A few months after the attack I remember watching a television documentary on the New York Fire Department. It was a documentary that touched me deeply. More than anything else, it was the fear that struck me. You could see it in their faces as they entered Tower One and set up their control. In the midst of the calm their overwhelming feelings of fear could not be hidden or denied. I felt their fear as I heard by way of the film the sound of the people falling from above and landing with that unmistakable thud. I watched as they pushed past the fear in the attempt to control a situation that was so out of control. It comes from the profession.

As I watched, I wondered all the while if I would be able to deal with what they had. I thought, if I can live out my whole career and never have to deal with something like that, I will be a happy man.

My daughter Courtney was six years old at the time and wondered why bad people would crash planes and kill people they did not even know. By the time I was able to speak with her I couldn't shield her from this evil – not that I could have entirely. She had already been affected. The overwhelming image that had stuck with her was that Middle Eastern people were bad people. We talked a lot. We talked particularly about racism. She needed to know that not all people from other countries were bad – in fact most were just like us – they wanted peace and happiness for their families. We talked about the fact that there are some people in the world who do very bad things. Courtney was a child learning a lesson before its time. I regretted her having to experience this education at such a young age, with the vivid images she had been exposed to.

Personally, this experience exposed my own racial prejudices. I had not really given much thought to how I felt about Muslims before then. Now I realized that I had unintentionally seen them in a negative frame and that was just wrong. Some Muslims had created terror, but these were only a small number who were in no way indicative of the true beliefs and values of the majority. The Muslim culture had seemed too far away, another world almost, for me to have to deal with my feelings about them. But September 11th forced me to come face to face with my own prejudice. So, instead of becoming more so, I exposed and overcame it.

This is an all too important lesson we must learn from this horrific attack – we must find ways to understand one another. There are major roadblocks to this understanding. If these are not removed then the attacks of September 11th are only a beginning. I watched news clips shortly after the attack that showed children in the Middle East cheering the act of terrorism. Just as my own daughter's mind was being filled with prejudice because of this, so too were theirs'. This could be repeated over and over again in our history unless we make an effort to understand one another. This is an educational issue that must be taken up.

I wonder, where does the responsibility for this lie? In us all, I think. In our governments, our schools, our businesses and in our media. We all need to take up the cause of understanding.

Today, I appreciate what I have more than I did before September 11th. I am thankful that we live in a country that is safe. Yet too, I am ever aware that the threat is much closer to home than at any other time in history. We are very blessed not to have to live in danger day by day, a way of life for many in the world. We must never take this for granted and we must work at understanding others to keep it.

Drawing by: Adriana Turner, Grade 6, The Study, Westmount Quebec - *Two Flags United*

Chapter 14

Ready, Aye, Ready!

Lt. Commander M.A. Morris: A Member of the Armed Forces

Lieutenant-Commander M.A. Morris is the Commanding Officer of the Naval Reserve Division, HMCS Cabot stationed with the Canadian Armed Forces at St. John's, Newfoundland. "Ready, aye, ready" is their motto and describes their attitude of heart and spirit.

I will never laugh at military exercise planners ever again! The military is famous for having us run drills on seemingly unrealistic and implausible scenarios. If one of the planners had come to me before September 11th, and said we were going to run an exercise to deal with 5,000 passengers on more than 2 dozen grounded transatlantic jets, with a hurricane, a plane crash and child pornography thrown in besides, I know we'd have laughed. But it was all those implausible exercises that prepared us for that week that none of us will ever forget.

It was a week when all our plans were suspended, even lost—training at Cabot, carpentry work at home, thousands of people expecting to see family or friends or colleagues—and yet it was a week out of all our lives when we gained such things as we never could have imagined, and bonds formed that will never break.

The day began like any other. I was in my office having a routine chat with the Military Police. One of the staff came 'round, asking if we'd heard the news, a plane crashed into the World Trade Center?

At first, we thought it was an accident—terrible enough—a small plane gone astray. But as the second plane hit, and then Washington, and Pennsylvania, we all realized it was an attack.

You know, a soldier's life is just like the old saying: "Ninety-nine per cent preparation; one per cent intense action." You see these things on the news, you drill on what you might do, then one day you're called upon to do it. You never know what the enemy will throw at you—a bomb, a jet-filled plane, or 5,000 stranded passengers—you just need to be ready, and to act.

Right away, I knew two things. I knew this was one of those defining moments in history, those rare moments when you'll forever remember where you were when it happened, and when we would all be tested on how we acted. And I knew too that we would be called on to serve, to act, not just to sit on the sidelines.

My first call wasn't to my family or friends—neither were my second or third calls!—but to my XO [executive officer] to begin to act. U.S. air space was being closed, scores of planes were in transit unable to reach their destinations, we must expect some would land here. Were we ready? What did we need to do?

We began to make calls to all Ship's Company personnel, and to the Cadet Detachment as well, to determine their availability to assist and to include them in preparations. Our people began to pour in, personal plans and commitments of all types abandoned without a second thought. Some ended up staying all week, people who in more routine times would be eager to leave work and head home, now slaving over mounds of laundry hidden in the back or preparing meals in the galley hour after hour, hidden from view and appreciation, with not a single complaint.

Our supply tech and galley staff hustled out to stock up on supplies and groceries; they came back with the longest cash register tape I think I've ever seen! Duty watches had to be established and a registration process designed. A visit was made to the airport to make sure that the emergency management team knew that our resources were ready and available whenever they were needed.

The official tasking didn't come through 'til early that evening, but by then the conversion was well along. During the summer, our facility serves as a cadet training camp, and we transform the classrooms into dormitories with bunk beds, and the galley into a 24-hour dining room with extra seating. Usually it takes us quite a few days to do the conversion, but this time, all hands on deck completed the task before the first busload pulled in!

The passengers were exhausted, frustrated, disoriented, confused . . . numbed. They'd been kept on board their planes for 8 or 10 hours some of them, then brought over to Mile One Stadium where the St. John's Command Centre was located. Every effort was made to keep planeloads together: if the passengers began to separate, it would be almost impossible to get them back together for rerouting.

Our first planeload was Delta 125, mostly Americans. Their first priority was the news: what was happening? We set up three TVs in the mess hall and the passengers tuned them all to CNN. Many of them stayed up all night, huddled by the blue light of the TV, thirsting for knowledge.

Of course, there were huge line-ups for payphones. The Ship's Company opened up our office phones, and had additional lines installed the next day. The Cadets set up computers for e-mail access. The Americans were overwhelmed by the attacks, but most began to relax once they were able to reach their loved ones and grasp the news.

Not all were so fortunate. The actress, Marisa Berensen, was on one of the flights grounded in St. John's, and learned that her sister, a well-known photographer, had been a passenger on one of the planes that was crashed into the World Trade Center. Her mother was left alone in Europe, and no one wanted her to hear this news from the TV or to be unconnected with loved ones. Our padre spent a lot of time with her, and we did whatever we could to ensure she was able to speak with her mother and comfort her. It certainly brought the pain of the attacks to us in a much more personal way, and reminded us of the importance of our duty as soldiers and sailors.

Two Sabena flights followed. My XO, Padre and I met each planeload, welcoming them and giving them as much of a briefing as we could. These passengers, mostly Europeans, while also upset and frustrated, are nonetheless more used to this kind of terrorist attack on their soil, and the necessity of security precautions and identity checks. In some ways, they viewed this moment in history as the time that ended our North American false sense of security, our detachment from Europe and Asia. People have been talking about us being one global village for some time now; but this was the day when we truly joined the global village for real, and for good.

Initially, language barriers prevented some of these passengers from communicating with us, but between the Ship's Company and other passengers, we eventually found a language match for each one.

An older Greek couple, who spoke no English, somehow bonded with a young officer Cadet Walsh, who spoke no Greek. The Greek man turned out to have been quite an athlete — a world champion and Olympic competitor. He had brought with him from the plane a small scrapbook with photos and clippings from his illustrious career (the passengers weren't supposed to bring even hand baggage off the planes, but he either hadn't understood the instructions, or had decided that he would not part with this scrapbook, this book of memories of his life). They would sit in the mess looking through the book together, talking and laughing, communicating in some way about sports and competition and a different side of life. On one page was a newspaper clipping from 1949, with an article and photo of this fellow in the prime of his sports career breaking a record. The article right next to it was about Newfoundland joining Confederation! Cadet Walsh was even more surprised to hear that the Greek is a member of the organizing committee for the 2004 Olympics in Athens, and invited him over for Greek hospitality and front-row seats! In this unpredictable time, a bond was forged that bridged an ocean and two generations.

One French passenger showed a lot of interest in our naval combat gear. It's what we wear around the base: strong, comfortable, and maybe a little stylish! This fellow pleaded with us to lend him one of these shirts, and we did. He turned out to be a Paris fashion designer who wanted to feature this idea in the next season's fashions! In the middle of adversity, opportunity often appears unexpectedly.

A Dutch couple were not alone when they admitted to not knowing where they were or what to expect. They recalled seeing a National Geographic special on icebergs, and that was their only reference, their only picture of Newfoundland. In fact, one of the most common responses of relatives when they heard from the diverted passengers was: "You're where?!?"

The couple had been carrying pocket knives, of great nostalgic value, but of course they weren't allowed back on the plane with them. Instead, they handed them to Cadet LeDrew, someone they'd befriended here, as a gift. Once they'd flown off, though, he couldn't keep them, so packaged them up and sent them back to the extremely grateful and surprised couple. I am so proud of the way our young men and women just kept giving of themselves, yet perhaps in the end it is us who have received the greater gifts, and gained an experience that will serve as a foundation throughout our careers in the armed forces.

A girl from South America was traveling alone, just with her cello. During her stay with us, her cello consumed her thoughts; it was her only concern. Would it be damaged? Lost? Stolen? The two were safely reunited when the airport finally reopened. It is the little things that often count the most during testing times. We can't do a lot about the big things, but can wrap our arms around the right-sized object, be it a cello, a family member or close friend.

The first night, we'd been told to expect 157, and had that many bunk beds made up with linen, but we had over 270 that night. We hurriedly set up air mattresses and sleeping bags on the floor. Of the hundreds of people that stayed with us during the week, with numerous nationalities, ages, dietary needs, economic means, expectations, dashed plans and discomforts, we had not a single complaint, not a single incident. The enemy threw us hundreds of passengers and we stood shoulder to shoulder, and prevailed.

The airport opened up again on Thursday September 13th, with flights able to return to Europe but not on to the U.S. Many passengers agreed to head back, but quite a few others decided to stay until their air carrier could get them to the U.S. As a result of this splitting of planeloads, we received several new buses of people on Thursday night to take the place of the departed Sabena passengers.

The people of St. John's responded with characteristic hospitality. Boxes of clothes and toys began to arrive right away. Both the Salvation Army and the Red Cross responded with basic toiletries, towels and other necessities. The boxes most appreciated by the passengers were brought over by The Atlantic Lottery Corporation: full of socks and underwear. Well, I thought, someone over there must have been stranded without their luggage to think of that!

Families from town drove over and invited stranded passengers home for a meal and a visit. On the third day, we gave passengers harbour tours in an effort to break their boredom and give them a taste of Canada. One American war veteran had had 6 hip replacements, so couldn't make it down the ladder into the boat. So we stretched regulations a bit and winched the boat up to him. He was absolutely thrilled, and his smile had to be a mile wide. A soldier always sticks with a fellow soldier. And a soldier always does what has to be done to get the job done.

Friday brought more surprises. The tail end of Hurricane Erin moved up the east coast, bringing steadily increasing winds and heavy rain. The deteriorating weather threatened to close the airport again, yet ultimately, when the airport did shut down it wasn't due to weather.

So many large planes had been diverted to St. John's that the apron was full and parked planes overflowed onto the runways, leaving only one runway open for takeoffs and landings. A small cargo plane crashed while trying to take off on this runway. Fortunately the two person crew was unharmed, but debris and fuel were scattered across the runway, closing the airport once more. It was quite a sight! All those wide-bodied planes lined up side to side like so many little toys. And a crashed plane besides. Like a child's game gone wrong.

There was a further incident at the airport that day, too. A foreign national was caught with child pornography in his luggage. That caused a bit of stir—insult to injury—but the authorities detained him and we all kept focused on the task at hand.

We did pause on Friday, though, as did so many around the world, for a memorial service. Passengers joined our company and cadets on the jetty as our Padre led the touching service. Ships in harbour blew their whistles as Cabot's bell was struck and we stood together for three minutes of silence.

Each one kept his or her own solace, yet we all stood together on the jetty with a palpable sense of shared loss, of sudden injury, and of new unity.

The weather cleared on Saturday as quickly as it had closed in, and crews moved in to clean up the remains of the cargo plane and ready the airport for more departures, this time to the U.S. as well.

"All your people are angels," one of the grateful passengers said to me as we embraced on her departure. Well, I thought, you might not say that if you read my disciplinary logs! Sensing my thoughts, she smiled a wise smile and added, "Angels to us." Adversity brings out the best in people.

The last passengers left on Sunday evening and we were left with just the clean up and the memories. Until the mail started arriving . . . flowers, coffee mugs, books, a tray of dried fruit, phone calls and e-mails, lots of thank you letters with photos of passengers reunited with their loved ones, enough to fill our own scrapbook at HMCS Cabot. And all around the world, passengers who were unexpectedly diverted to Newfoundland are proudly wearing HMCS Cabot caps to the unknowing looks of their families, who can only imagine what that week was like for them and for us.

I will never laugh at military planners again. It was so rewarding finally to be able to act, the exercises behind us. It was a traumatic week in every way, but the most enriching many of us will know. That week witnessed the greatest team-building I have ever known: old got to know new, senior got to know junior, all of us got to know the drills and facilities like the back of our hands, and got to know each other even better.

All our lives we had trained for something, we knew not what, and then it came and we just acted the way we had been trained and the way we were expected to. We are there for when bad things happen, and a terrible thing did happen, and so many good things have grown out of that.

The enemy threw his worst terrorist attack against us. And how did we react? We opened our base, we opened our homes, we opened our hearts to strangers. And they will never be strangers again. We did our jobs as soldiers and sailors—and our brothers and sisters are still toiling across the globe—and ended the week as friends.

"When Daddy leaves for war...after he left you started to grow, when he comes home, if he comes home, you've grown too much to cuddle."

Poem and Drawing by: Logan Jackson, Grade 4, Warburg School, Warburg, Alberta

Chapter 15

To Survive, To Learn, To Lead

Peter Dey: An Executive

Peter Dey is best known as Canada's leading champion of excellence in corporate governance. He chaired the original 1994 Toronto Stock Exchange Committee that introduced Canada's Corporate Governance Guidelines in its hard-hitting and ground-breaking report "Where Were The Directors?" Peter was formerly the Chairman and Managing Director of Morgan Stanley Canada, and a member of the board of directors of its Manhattan-based parent, Morgan Stanley. Recently, Peter rejoined his law firm Osler, Hoskins & Harcourt as partner.

My office is on the 66th floor of First Canadian Place in downtown Toronto. On a normal day, I would stand at the window and look out over the heart of the business district, the towers of the big banks, the venerable Royal York Hotel and Union Station, the ribbon of the Gardiner Expressway, the revitalized Harbourfront beyond, and beyond that, Toronto Harbour, Centre Island with its tiny airport, the vastness of Lake Ontario, and on a clear day, the Niagara Peninsula on the far side of the lake, and the mist from Niagara Falls itself pluming up above the escarpment.

A few weeks after September 11th, though, my colleague and I were standing at my window and we saw none of that. We were looking straight down, debating what we would actually do if it happened here, what options we really had.

My colleague was in favour of buying "office parachutes", the new hot-selling item for office tower workers. If we broke the window and leapt out just far enough, the parachutes would open and we would flutter gently down to King Street far below—at least that was the theory. I craned my neck and pushed my nose against the glass, and could just make out the strip of street almost covered by taxis, cars, streetcars and pedestrians. I wasn't so sure.

If we could only get over to the roof of the Toronto-Dominion Centre, I thought, then they could rescue us from there. It was only a dozen or so floors beneath us, and just across King Street, perhaps 50 or 60 feet. I shook my head. I couldn't jump across King Street on the ground; I'm not going to be able to jump 50 feet in the air, parachute or no parachute.

After studying the options, I chose to get on with my life, as did everyone else on the floor.

I've always been interested in the concept of leadership. In fact, I've spent a lot of my life understanding what sets leaders apart, why we look up to them and follow them. A strong sense of values, a commitment to learning, a willingness to take a stand: these are some of the qualities I've found.

September 11th was one of those rare days when we will not only remember where we were the moment we found out, but what we were doing and even wearing.

I was still in my workout clothes, having just come in from a workout. We keep the radio on CBC in the kitchen, and the announcer was saying: "My goodness! A plane has just gone into the World Trade Center!"

I immediately turned on CNN, to get informed, and stayed in front of the screen for much of the next 3 hours, watching history unfold before my eyes.

"It must have been an errant commuter plane," observed the commentator on CNN. I couldn't believe that: it was such a clear day, no commuter pilot could have wandered so far astray as to collide with a skyscraper errantly.

Two things were simultaneously going through my mind: a deep concern for colleagues and friends, and a need to get the facts. I called friends at Morgan Stanley in Toronto, to communicate my concern and to find out the extent of the impact on Morgan Stanley globally. The investment banking arm is located in midtown Manhattan, but the brokerage arm occupied 20 floors of the second tower of the World Trade Center. Further, Morgan Stanley's President was also at the World Trade Center for meetings.

My next call was to my own office, where by then the decision had already been made to give employees the day off. U.S. airspace was closed, planes were being diverted to Canada, and there was a general sense of uncertainty and anxiety. My assistant brought my day's work with her out to the street where I met her. It was an eerie scene, the office towers emptying and all those people with so many unanswered questions.

I got home in time to meet my daughter coming home from school. We spent some time together, my wife, daughter and myself, trying to make some sense of it all.

The first thing was to get the facts straight. My daughter had heard some things in school, but they had not really understood what had happened. After the facts, though, came the harder part, trying to understand what possible motives could result in the events of September 11th. Then to understand the broader implications for the western world and our way of life.

We talked late into the night about fanaticism and how evil people try to disguise their true nature with religious precepts. Yes, there are different ways of life from ours, and a vast misunderstanding between those ways of life. There are gaps at both the spiritual and economic level, and those were exposed on September 11th like never before.

How then should we respond to this? Our conclusions were to understand the gross disparities, the different ways of life, and the products of that. Be curious, embrace learning, lifelong learning. Find out everything that you can about others.

But understand something else just as true. There will always be extremists in the world, who will find an excuse to carry out violent acts. Practice tolerance for the ways of others, yes, that is central to our values. But do not tolerate evil and violence, whatever their guise. Take a stand against it, oppose it.

And of course two more understandings were reinforced that terrible day. I was already sensitive to the fragility of life—as one journeys through life, one comes face-to-face with mortality more often—but September 11th certainly reinforced that. And it reinforced the importance of family and close friends. Since then, I think we've all been more communicative, and more sensitive, within our families and circle of close relations and friends.

Late that same day, September 11th, I called a good friend of mine in San Francisco. "I'm signing up for bomber duty" was his response. There was a lot of anger that day, on both sides.

From e-mails and telephone calls over the next couple of days, it became clear what had happened at the World Trade Center. Of twenty floors full of employees, Morgan Stanley lost six, six lives ended suddenly and tragically.

It could have been—would have been—much worse, but for one person. The head of security for Morgan Stanley at the World Trade Center had been there in 1993 when terrorists set off a truck bomb in the basement in an attempt to bring the towers down. Since then, he and the heads of security for employers at WTC spent many hours developing contingency plans, practicing evacuations, preparing for another emergency.

On September 11th, he led the evacuation at Morgan Stanley, rounding people up, calming them down, directing them to the stairwells and the way to survival. He escorted the last ones down to safety on the streets below, and turned to look at the burning tower. I'm going back up, he announced, to check the floors for stragglers, for any one who had failed to hear the instructions or stayed at their desk, for whatever reason. That was the last any one saw of him, heading up the stairwells of the second tower seeking to save one more life.

We deeply regret the loss of even a single life, Morgan Stanley's CEO wrote to us by e-mail. Under the circumstances, we can only be grateful that the toll was not higher. We will survive.

I was scheduled to fly to Budapest later that week, for OECD meetings on governance. They were understanding when I called to postpone my trip. It wasn't long before I boarded a plane again, though. It's become such a big part of our lives. If we want to be privileged to lead, we have first to learn, and that means traveling, taking risks. This generation travels the world the way we traveled from Ottawa to Toronto. One of my stepsons was in Mongolia on September 11th, and my daughter will travel to every part of the globe and experience things we can barely imagine. September 11th won't change that, although it has changed the way we look at the same world.

Scarier even than returning to my office tower was flying again. When the flight attendant went running down the aisle, the first thing that ran through my head was, what are we going to do? The second thing was, she's probably going to get a pillow for someone! When the plane lands, and on our way out we thank the crew, we mean "thanks" in a completely different way than we did before. It used to be a sort of casual greeting, now it's heartfelt appreciation for returning to the job. They survived, they learned, and now they lead by example.

There was a memorial service late that week at Queen and Church for one of the Canadians who had lost their lives on September 11th. I didn't know him really well, but I did know him. I don't usually go to those things, but this time was different, and so I did. The service was beautifully done; it attracted a real cross-section of people, from different walks of life, yet sitting that September afternoon together in a church as one. It was so important to go; I'm so glad I did.

Later, I had the opportunity to participate in a memorial service event in Manhattan, where Mayor Guiliani spoke. It was a session where emotions were still exposed, and his vision and humanity really impacted this group of corporate business people in a significant way. He spoke of this being the same world, but now we had more knowledge of our vulnerability and the strength of our values. The way the Mayor of New York City responded, on September 11th and since, has perhaps had the most impact on me. Here is an example of outstanding leadership at the time when the civilized world most needed leadership.

He didn't hesitate. He went into the centre of the storm and found out everything that he could. He risked his life. He led his people out. He turned and stood. He led by example, not expecting more of others than he was prepared to give. He was the servant of the people. He drew on his own beliefs and values, so firm a foundation that we all ended up standing on it together.

In many ways, September 11th was an attack on my way of life, on the things that I stand for. The World Trade Center was the heart of the global corporate community, and most of those who died were executives in service of global governance and trade. I have spent much of my energy traveling the globe advocating good governance as an essential component of a globalizing economy. Globalization has changed the world so dramatically and permanently, and my purpose had been to instill the principles of governance among its corporate leaders.

Now I faced a choice as I returned to my 66th floor office and stared out of its window. Should I step down? Were my efforts in vain? Should we concede defeat?

Far from it. September 11th emphasizes the importance of the work of people who, at various levels, are trying to reduce the gross disparities and bridge the glaring gaps so apparent in our world. I choose to continue my work, at the level of the shareholder, the boardroom and the executive, as my colleagues choose to continue theirs.

We have survived September 11th, and have been changed. We have learned, we have grown in understanding, I hope, and in wisdom. We will continue to go into the world, we will continue to learn, we will serve and teach and make every effort to provide leadership in global governance to leave a legacy for our daughters and sons.

Drawing By: Lauren Sarvas, Age 9, Grade 4, Warburg School, Warburg, Alberta

Chapter 16

Faith is the Key

Ann Lorenzen: A Mother

Ann Lorenzen is the mother of three—a 23 year old daughter, a 17 year old son and a 9 year old daughter—each of whom was impacted significantly but differently by the September 11th attacks. Ann is a Regina regulator and accountant who works to ensure the safety of credit union depositors' funds in Saskatchewan.

I was all by myself when I heard the news, which made it seem a bit unreal. On my way to work, I heard the news on my car radio. It reminded me of the way people reacted to the broadcast of H.G. Wells' *War of the Worlds* over the radio years ago: first disbelief, then a sense of horror overcame me.

The only thing I could think of doing was to pray: "Oh Lord, if this is true, please help." It was the same prayer I prayed when I heard of the Oklahoma City bombing, and the Columbine school shooting. When faced with devastation like this, the only person who could help is God.

When I got to work, I went down to the cafeteria, and there it was on the big screen TV. I just watched and watched and watched, in a numb state. When you *saw* it, you knew it must be real.

It was like the most graphic war movies—*The Killing Fields* or *Schindler's List*—when things turn horrible right there in front of your eyes. I felt an ache in my heart, in my inner being. I was profoundly shaken to the core at the depth of horror and devastation. Part of me wanted to be angry, mad at someone for doing this, but I couldn't get angry, or even speak about it.

But, just like those movies, part of your brain rejects such traumatic events. I sat down with my work associates, but they didn't want to talk about the incident. They went back to work, speechless, in denial, even shock, trying to make things seem normal, to will things back to normal.

Of course, my thoughts quickly turned to my kids. How would they react? How would they respond? Would they be bitter? Hateful? Or would their spirits soar above it? I didn't want them to be afraid—fear can dominate people's minds and immobilize them. What could I possibly say to help them?

Start by turning to God. Listen to the still small voice inside you. Call on God to help you soar above this instead of being devastated. Asking for divine intervention has a practical advantage, as well: it keeps people from reacting too quickly and rashly. It gives you time to assimilate rather than lashing out in hate and revenge. Better to pray, reflect, and react with wisdom and deliberation.

When things get so rough that you realize you don't have control, then focus on what you can control instead of worrying about what you can't. After days like September 11th, the most important thing is one's own attitude; how we choose to face circumstances. Choose to react in the right way, in stride, allowing yourself to move forward, learn and grow, not to react in hate and anger.

For my son, Nicholas, I prayed that there wouldn't be a full-scale military response. Nicholas and I watched a TV show about a Newfoundland battalion that was sent to war, and suffered over 700 casualties. My friends and I thought about our sons being sent to war. Nicholas was 17, and until that day, I never thought that I would have to live through a war and the chance of my son being taken in that way. For the first few days after September 11th, I waited for the next attack, and the next after that, and for the reactions. If it did go on, how could we possibly stop the escalation? That could be the end for all of us.

We got a little more comfortable each day as the next attack didn't come, and the response seemed more measured. It seemed remarkable that there wasn't another attack. You just had a sense of foreboding, that several more attacks were planned and waiting to be executed. Waiting for something else to happen was like a suspense movie, where you just know it isn't over yet. But the sense of heaviness began to lift after several months went by without the other shoe dropping. Perhaps the worst is over, I thought.

We had lost our sense of security and safety. But there was no sense worrying about it, about the next Orange Alert or anthrax scare or who might be sitting next to you on the plane. We can't prepare ahead anyway. We can't see what lies ahead.

That reinforces the importance of faith and our attitude inside: after all, that is what we can prepare. That is what we have control over.

My 9 year old daughter had a lot of questions. She was all right as long as we gave her honest answers. We prayed together; prayer was her outlet. She needed someone to talk to and to express herself and her feelings to.

I explained that the attack was a bad thing, and our logical reaction would be to hate, yet we must rise above it. No matter what someone does to you, it is important to do the right thing yourself, and leave the rest to God. It's always harder to find grace and forgiveness when it happens to us.

Her biggest concern was for those directly affected. How could we help them? The opportunity to help gave her hope, and lifted her hopelessness. We always talk about reaching out to those less fortunate. Here was an opportunity to turn her love into action, and she kept giving as much away and sharing as much as she could, with organizations that were helping. There have always been—and will always be—wars and evil; we do what we can.

My 23 year old daughter didn't verbalize as much. She was deeply affected by the reality, and dealt with it more quietly, in her own sphere at university. She didn't watch the TV coverage as much as the rest of us.

It reached a point when the rest of us caught up with her; when we had had enough coverage of September 11th and its aftermath. There was just so much news and context of Middle East politics and history; evening after evening of news and documentaries.

Different people respond differently in the same circumstances. My husband was ready to move on much more quickly. Both family and work took much more time before we were ready. At work, they brought in counsellors over the noon hour to speak with staff. Some staff thought it was an over-reaction. But quite a few took advantage of it, and really appreciated it.

Since September 11th, my thoughts have often returned to why. I made efforts to return to a normal life. After the shock and numbness, there was a tremendous sense of fear, a loss of personal safety and control. I felt vulnerable, exposed, mortal, helpless. Later, I searched for ways to take control: airline security checks, regulations . . . the regulator in me took over for a while, but my husband pointed out we don't have that control I was seeking.

A lot of good has come out of September 11th, for me and many others.

I realized that, in my own life, I had taken so many steps to control my destiny. Since September 11th, I've learned that you can't do that, and you can't live governed by fear either.

We witnessed heroism and compassion in so many others in the following days, people motivated to do something, reaching out to others, putting others' needs ahead of their own.

I have a tremendous sense of empathy for the burdens others bear. There are a lot of things that can happen in life that are more challenging to hope than one's own death: the death of a loved one; the permanent impairment of one's own life, like being paralyzed from the neck down. I've gone through similar, but much smaller, things, and it's like being in a tunnel; you just have to keep going. The light at the end of the tunnel is the only hope. I'm thankful that we haven't had to live through a war: this is one single catastrophe, but for the most part we aren't exposed to that kind of trauma. We are very privileged to live in Canada. I look at South Africa and the AIDS crisis there, all that devastation with no end in sight. There but by the grace of God go I . . . when I was growing up in Venezuela, I saw a lot of poor kids, and I asked God if we could be happy if we faced that life and those bleak circumstances with no way out? Could we put one foot in front of the other and keep moving forward? I pray that people would have it in their hearts to just keep going.

I wake up each morning now with a renewed sense of hope, that we're on the planet for a purpose and for a finite time, for however long we get, and we must have an eternal perspective, not just focus on the here and now. It's actually easier for me to fly now; I have accepted my fate.

My message to my own kids, and the next generation: faith is the real key in surviving loss and setback. Choose to hope: there is a plan for your life, you are here for a purpose, life is precious but brief: it can be gone in the blink of an eye, whether you are 80 years old or 6. Maintain an eternal perspective, otherwise life may seem empty and futile. You never know what's going to happen here, so focus on the positive and on knowing what lies beyond this life. Both are a gift, and both are worthwhile!

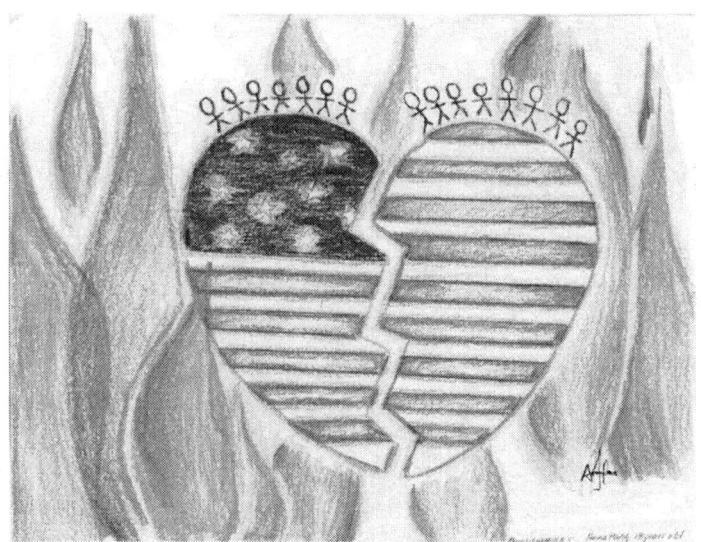

Drawing By: Anna Pang, Age 13, Bayview Hill E. S., Richmond Hill, Ontario

Chapter 17

50/50 Hindsight

Captain John MacNeil - A Firefighter

No community was affected as deeply by September 11th as the firefighters. Every firehouse was affected, not just those in New York City. John MacNeil is a Fire Captain at the 15th Station of the Halifax Fire Department.

We were on duty at the fire station that morning of September 11th, completely unaware of what was unfolding just down the coast from us. The phone rang—someone told us that a plane had flown into the World Trade Center—so we turned on CNN and the whole crew watched it together.

We had talked about fighting highrise fires many times before, about what to do, the risks and dangers. As the fire at the twin towers raged in front of our eyes, we thought the fire would go on forever. We did not think the towers would collapse. Our thoughts were for getting as many people out as possible. Our fellow firefighters and policemen in New York City were clearly thinking exactly the same things.

When the first tower collapsed, we all knew that the second would as well; it was just a matter of time. Our thoughts turned to the firefighters now: how many of them must have just died in this collapse?

For some time we were in complete shock, just stunned. It was like a bad movie, but all too real. One firefighter who'd been on driving training missed that morning, and didn't believe any of us when we told him; he thought it was just a sick joke.

Our thoughts turned to the immediate future. What's next? More attacks? And what response? We knew this wasn't done. Would we all shortly be embroiled in a war? Would it be World War III?

Slowly, events began to come into focus. All those passengers who got onto planes in Boston, Washington and Newark had no idea their planes would be flown into the World Trade Center, the Pentagon and a field in Pennsylvania. 3,000 innocent lives were lost that morning. What a terrible shame that, 5,000 miles away from the Middle East, people in the U.S.A. had to pay this price.

Firefighters are very much like a second family, as tight as brothers. I remember losing 6 one night in Worcester. We sent a delegation to that funeral service, thinking it was the worst it could ever get. Then 350 firefighters were killed at the World Trade Center on September 11th.

Fire stations have their own lingo: one expression we have is "hindsight is 50/50." We say that rather than "20/20" because hindsight is just that much sharper and keener than any foresight can ever be.

After September 11th, we had plenty of time for 50/50 hindsight. We all re-evaluated how to fight fires in highrise buildings and office towers. Yes, we likely would change the location of the command post. But I expect firefighters would go in again: I've spoken with firefighters in New York City, and while management is cautioning they might not go in next time, we all know that we would. That's our job: we have to go in and help. The nature of the job is that you could lose your life in any fire—you could go into a house fire and worry about the floor collapsing and hesitate going in . . . if it's your time to go, if the big fellow is calling your name, then there is nothing you can do about it.

My message to the next generation? September 11th shows us that violence is not the answer; it's no way to solve things. Give peace a chance: I know, I sound like a 1970's hippie, but the Irish fought for 400 years over Protestant/Catholic troubles, Israelis and Palestinians have been fighting for even longer over a narrow strip of desert, Iraqis and Kuwaitis fought over oil. I thought our generation would learn from these, and from the hard experiences of Vietnam, and pursue peace, but now here we are again, fighting a war on terrorism.

I'm not optimistic about peace. So much is going on out of our view that leads to war, to retaliation and to revenge. People are motivated by greed in every part of the world. Is it money or oil that makes the world go 'round instead of peace and understanding? September 11th is just one more escalation in a hundreds of years old conflict. No generation has learned from the mistakes of the previous one. Instead, each one personalizes its own hate. Will the next generation? Will yours?

With every tragedy, you can always find some benefits: 350 firefighters didn't die for nothing, and we all need to look for the benefits 50/50 hindsight brings.

Firefighters ourselves are much tighter than ever before. In 1996, they amalgamated the old Halifax, Dartmouth, Sackville and Coal Harbour detachments into the new Halifax Fire Department. There had been some tensions and divisions ever since with the newly intertwined force. But since September 11th, we all feel a much closer bond; we've all joined together as one. It's the common experience that we've all lived through.

The relationship with the public has been unbelievable since September 11th. Firefighters are held in the highest esteem ever—I haven't heard one negative word about firefighters since then. The media, too, has had nothing bad to say: they've been championing firefighters to the public. People come up and want to shake your hand, just because you're a firefighter. It's both good and bad being the most trusted profession—sometimes I just don't want to say I'm a firefighter because of all the public interest, support and attention.

Halifax is a major port—a lot of things go through here—so you never know what will happen. New security measures may stop more plane hijackings, but terrorists will choose a different method next time. We had the Swiss Air disaster here too. It was a very difficult experience for Halifax firefighters, very gory. Some firefighters don't want to see things like that again. None of the crew have changed their plans about their career; although some of the senior guys have been looking at retirement, so far it's just talk.

September 11th put a damper on things for a while, but each of us has decided, has chosen, to go on. Personally, I choose to live life: if it's going to happen, it's going to happen. I choose to keep on living. The summer after September 11th, we finally took the plunge and went trekking in Nepal. We'd been talking about it for years, but now I can say, with 50/50 hindsight, we've done it!

Drawing By: Kayla McWhinney, Grade 5, St. Mary's, Goderich, Ontario

Chapter 18

Take Comfort

Rita MacNeil: A Singer Song-Writer

Rita MacNeil is a singer songwriter well known to most Canadians. Rita shares with us the source of her strength and her poetic wisdom on hope, love and her dreams for future generations.

It was September 11th, 2001 and I was scheduled to perform that night in Windsor, Ontario, a border town, directly across from Detroit, Michigan. That morning, I was still in my hotel room in London, Ontario when the telephone rang. It was my son, Wade. He just kept saying "it's awful, it's just so awful!!!"

It took some time to figure out just what was wrong. What had made him so upset? Had something happened in the family? To him? Was this just some sort of practical joke? He was just so upset. Eventually I made some sense of the call, hung up the phone and turned on the television. All I could do was cry. I felt paralyzed, and consumed with a numbness and deep shock that I had never experienced in my life.

All I wanted to do was to go home. I just wanted to go home. So I did the next best thing, I called home to Cape Breton and talked with my loved ones. The need to be with people was overwhelming to me. I contacted my band members and talked with them so I did not feel so alone.

As happens with me, my immediate response was to internalize my feelings in a song. I called it ...

Take Comfort.

I can now well imagine how this came to be
How a glimpse of your darkness
Brought the changes we see
Yet for all of the sadness
You spread just like fire
We are moved by the spirit
That rose in the night

Now I no longer trust the sea when it's calm
The sky when it's blue or the heart of all men
Or the birds flying high or the peace that I knew
But I know in my life I take comfort in you

I can weep for a neighbour
I can weep for a friend
And I'll cry for the goodness you've taken away
But there's one other journey
We'll all meet again
Carry home all the weary
To peace once again

Now I no longer trust the sea when it's calm
The sky when it's blue or the heart of all men
Or the birds flying high or the peace that I knew
But I know in my life I take comfort in you

There's a bell in the city
That chimes around noon
And a choir that's singing
A song I once knew
I will take time to listen
for it's there I'll take heart
And take comfort in others
When the hours grow dark

Now I no longer trust the sea when it's calm
The sky when it's blue or the heart of all men
Or the birds flying high or the peace that I knew
But I know in my life I take comfort in you

I went on to do the concert that evening and am so glad I did. In my heart I knew I had to be there. To be with people – together we were able to get through the night. Together we could begin to hope again.

Without hope there is nothing. And, there are a number of things I hope we will remember about that day. First, that we set our priorities on the most important things in life. For me, those are love and family and it is those I choose to focus on as my priorities. Since September 11th, I am even more aware of this and the significant issues of life than ever.

We should remember empathy. At times I still feel such deep sadness. And then there is the fear. I feel such empathy for others – those who were in New York and Washington and the fear they must have felt and continue to feel. This event shook me and us all at our foundations. I have always been someone of deep compassion – but that is now forever heightened.

And then there is depth of spirit and courage. I will remember the wonderful spirit that came from such horror - people pulling together, helping each other, loving one another.

I hope that we will remember to value peace. I hope that we will remember the good that comes out of this — hate is a powerful emotion — love is stronger.

And what of the next generation? My own children were deeply affected by the events of September 11th. My hope for them and for all who follow us is that as a people we won't forget. There is so often a rush to get on with life — but we are changed now and we can't — nor should we rush on without due reflection. We must take time to remember. And then, we must keep on from what we have learned. Prevention comes from remembrance.

"I still feel sad, but I am better. I am OK but I wish I was better."

Drawing By: Madison Littman, Grade 4, Warburg School, Warburg, Alberta

Chapter 19

We Will Remember and Prevail

Bob Chester: A Pilot

Bob Chester has been flying for 18 years, including the last 5 for Air Canada. As with all of our interviews, these views are Bob's personally, and not those of his employer or anyone else. Based out of Toronto, Bob makes his home outside Ottawa.

It was a clear evening as I nosed the Air Canada jet up from the runway at Newark. As we cleared the New Jersey coast, we turned left towards Canada and, as we so often did, flew over the twin towers of the World Trade Center. I looked down at the city and admired how beautiful the towers looked in the last rays of the setting sun.

It was September 10th, and the next morning, the towers would be gone in a cloud of dust.

Off duty at home the following morning, I was listening to National Public Radio when the news came in that a plane had hit the World Trade Center. Initially, we all thought it was an accident. When you're being vectored around, you do sometimes get close to the World Trade Center, so it's conceivable you could run into it, if it was foggy.

I turned on the TV. It was obviously a perfectly clear day. Announcers were discussing the size of the plane, speculating that it had been a small plane. One look at the amount of damage on the side of the tower showed that this was clearly a large plane, and this was no accident.

The second plane hit. Actually you could see it being flown in: the pilot maneuvered it as it approached, turning at the last second. A cold, deliberate act, someone flying a commercial airliner into an office tower full of people.

The images on TV were so unreal, beyond what Hollywood could dream up. Images of planes being flown into buildings, firefighters and rescue workers running towards the burning buildings moments before they collapsed on them.

That morning, I, like so many of us, was trying to understand what was going on. Obviously, there are people in the world who hate us; their hate was lived out in front of our eyes, as their character was illuminated by their choice of targets (office towers full of workers) and weapons (civilian planes full of passengers and fuel). My immediate concern was for our Air Canada crews, both those on duty and off: New York City and Washington were common layovers for both.

Then they closed our airspace, raising a whole series of new questions. Where will they put all those planes? The options are rather limited. As the whole system shut down, many Air Canada crews were grounded that morning in various places, unable to get home. The Pennsylvania plane crash heightened my fears: how many more? What will the end result be?

I realized others would be wondering about me. After calling my wife at work, I called my brother and parents, reassuring them that I was at home and OK.

As I watched helplessly from home during the next couple of days, I was galled by the utter simplicity of the act itself, of hijacking the right planes, with few passengers and full gas tanks on a clear day, and turning them into weapons of mass destruction. How could the CIA and intelligence services *not* have an inkling of this? Osama Bin Laden has been their number one target for ten years, completely and openly dedicated to acts of terror against the U.S.A.

Yes I was angry, but my anger was a pilot's anger against these people hijacking airliners the way they did. From a pilot's point of view, hijacking has always been done for a reason—money, getting someone out of jail, publicity—never to destroy the plane using it as a weapon.

September 11th changed everyone's view of how to deal with a hijacked plane. Before then, everyone—police, military, air crew—would work together to do anything to help an airliner in distress. Now a hijacked airliner is seen as a pariah, a potential weapon aimed at a population centre—which is where the runways are. Now, police and military have to regard such an airliner as a potential weapon and therefore a potential target. To air crew, we simply *must* protect the flight deck: that is the way that we can keep the plane from hitting a target and causing mass destruction. That means securing the door physically, and making a conscious effort to be fully aware of who and what is around whenever opening the door.

In a way, the terrorists began to lose this battle on the morning of September 11th. The Pennsylvania plane was, from their point of view, a failure, a defeat. The people on board that plane who sacrificed their lives to re-take the flight deck from the terrorists scored the first victory in the new war. Now all of us—pilots, flight attendants and passengers—know exactly what we would do if it happened to us. We wouldn't like doing it, but we would all do it.

On the third day, airlines began to fly again. I went out to Halifax to fly an international flight home. All the planes were still lined up at the Halifax airport, and there were so many people wandering around town, people who never expected to be there. It was quite sombre at the airport: they were holding a memorial service that day. In spite of all the commotion and uncertainty, people were ensuring they took time to remember.

As I stood watching the participants, both staff and passengers, it was clear that there was a lot of uncertainty still. Many seemed to be in shock still: they had had no release since September 11th. As we shepherded them through the new security procedures, there was no anger, though; they were all very patient. Even now, it can be pretty tedious going through security, including matching each checked bag with each passenger, but people understand. Nobody wants a rogue bag or a rogue passenger.

The day to day working for pilots hasn't changed all that much, although we do have a heightened sense of awareness in observing passengers and the planes. Our clientele has changed: people no longer fly for fun or perks. The enjoyment aspect is gone, and even casual meetings don't call for flying. It is the seasoned traveller who needs to fly for business that makes up the bulk of today's clientele.

And the relationship between pilots and passengers has completely changed. Parents would bring their kids up to the flight deck, we'd give them trinkets and wow them with the dials and lights, and the view. Now the door is locked and barred. Passengers realize that this new reality is for their own safety and benefit, although we all feel the loss of innocence.

Since September 11th, flight crews on Air Canada and every other airline have returned to the air. Very few have left or retired early. Most of us just accept that this is all part of our job.

A few weeks after the attacks, I had a layover at La Guardia, and I went over to the firehouses of New York City. Each stands now like a silent shrine in memory of so many of their own who were killed. It's quite remarkable. There are lots of signs everywhere you go in the U.S.A.—flags, badges, pins, banners, even a picture or remembrance on the desk at work. They all say the same thing: we will remember and we will prevail.

Every day something new is happening: that's the nature of this new war, that's very tough to win and never really over. It's a horrendous enemy to fight because it's so hard to find. They don't wear uniforms, they hide from view and strike when and where they can. It's a beehive we've had to stick our nose into.

But we did not and cannot let this change us, change our way of life. We need to appreciate Canada and the U.S. and our freedom, much more keenly now: our freedom and values, our freedom of religion, freedom to travel. Al Qaeda was probably pretty surprised at our response, at our fortitude, at our unity: that we will remember and we will prevail.

Drawing By: Steven McDonnell, Grade 5, St. Mary's, Goderich, Ontario

Chapter 20

Father Mychal Judge

Eric Reguly – A Journalist

Eric is a business columnist for the Globe and Mail. He and his wife were particularly touched and affected by the horrific events of September 11th. On October 22nd, 1994 Father Mychal Judge, the chaplain of the New York Fire Department, married Eric and his wife. On September 11th, 2001, New York City named Father Judge "Victim Number One".

I arrived in the office early on that day – around 8:30 – the television was on. But I can't remember if it was turned to ROB TV, the Globe's own network or CNN. Frankly I did not pay too much attention, thinking it was an accident. When the second plane hit my colleague Margaret Wente was quick to exclaim "this is terrorism." My first thought was, "oh, what a great story!" It is the dispassionate journalist in me.

I made my way over to ROB TV where I soon discovered all of our producers glued to the screen. It was not long before I was asked, "do you want to go to New York?" I am after all a New Yorker at heart having lived there for five years. Panic ensued. The borders had been closed, airports shut down, we could not even charter a plane. We decided to drive. The first two cars left that day, I left the following day by car along with Jan Wong, a fellow columnist.

I called my wife. And then it hit me. This may be a personal story - we may have friends who died in the Towers. Little did we know that it would be the man who had married us!

The day moved on. It was around midnight, as I packed my bags, the news came. I was listening to the midnight news on CBC radio when Mayor Guiliani's voice announced that Father Mychal Judge had been killed. It struck me like a cannon ball in the stomach. My wife Karen had been saying all day that Father Judge would be dead. She knew that he would be there. He was always there — no matter the magnitude of the tragedy. Myself, I was sure he would be fine. After all, God was on his side — He always had been, and I assured myself, He would be this time too. I ran up from the basement of our home in the Beaches and told my wife. And then we just cried.

From our loaded van as we drove to New York, I called in my story about Father Mychal Judge.

Arriving in New York we left our van with friends in New Jersey and made the long walk into Manhattan. We checked in to the Metropolitan Club on Fifth Avenue where I am a member and began the next leg of our journey to Ground Zero. "Eerie" is only a glimpse of how the sights, sounds and smells can be described. The smell of the fires, the haze in the air and the streets empty but for police cars and emergency vehicles. Eerie.

Just as we approached Times Square a bomb scare was called in at the Empire State Building. Strange though, people did not run in panic. For the most part they just stood and stared at the building. Firemen arrived — not in shiny red fire engines but in their personal vehicles. They no longer had fire engines! Of course in the end it turned out to be a false alarm.

What I will remember most is turning the corner onto West 31st Street where Father Judge's church, St. Francis of Assisi, stands. His church is directly across from a fire station – a station that had lost several of its members. While Father Judge was the chaplain for the entirety of the New York fire department, this station stood out. Because of the proximity to the church, these were the men and women he met with for lunch most days.

As we rounded the corner, late into the evening, we encountered the most amazing scene. The firemen had towed their ladder truck back to the firehouse and parked it on the street between the two buildings. Its windows blown out, tires flattened, its body completely covered in dust, the truck had been transformed into a memorial to the Priest we all so deeply loved. Firemen, having worked non-stop for two days, were filthy, tired, torn and tattered. They gathered in groups crying together or just standing there having a smoke. Hundreds of people had gathered between the two buildings and had covered the truck with flowers and notes to him. It was a perfect scene of tragedy in miniature.

It was then I completely broke down. I called my wife on my cell phone, turned the journalist off and sobbed.

Friday was the remembrance service. It was a very private thing. Held in the church basement, to my surprise it was an open casket. The theory is that he was not hit by debris but by a jumper. To most accounts this appears to be true. I will never forget this service. I stepped up to his casket and said a prayer. As I stepped back and spent the next half hour or so just watching, I was moved by the friends who came to pay their respects. Many of them firemen, exhausted, dirty, red-eyed and tearful, each quietly taking their turn to step up to their friend's casket and say their private goodbyes and prayers.

The funeral on Saturday was clearly a celebrity funeral. The Mayor was there of course, the Clintons and any number of celebrities. There were thousands of people, flowers, trucks — only then did I realize just how loved this man was.

My wife is Jewish and I Catholic. That's why we met Father Judge, a Franciscan Monk. We were living in London at the time and wanted to be married in New York. It was our city. We wanted to be married in an inter-faith service, a service that would recognize both of our faiths. This is not as easily done as said. Ultimately I even needed to receive Papal dispensation for the wedding. We made a series of enquiries including to the United Nations, where we finally were directed to Father Mychal Judge, the Franciscan Monk, a street priest in New York who also happened to be Chaplain to the New York City fire department.

The Father was always in trouble with the church, often pushing the envelope and tradition. I remember doing confession with him. Not separated by a wooden wall but together, his hand on mine, he listened and we prayed. He was a delightful man. On our wedding day he arrived in his Fire Department cruiser, lights flashing. He dashed from the cruiser in his brown monk's robe with its white belt and his sandaled feet to lead our unique interfaith ceremony. Although we have kept in touch over the years, that day is the last time we saw him. We wanted to take our girls to meet him, to get to know him. We wanted a Priest in their lives and we wanted it to be him. September 11ᵗʰ changed all that.

He was a gentle man yet, a real-life action figure. He was an action man. I recall the story from the 1970's when he was called to a home in New Jersey. A husband and father was inside with a gun and his family and his intention was to kill them all. The police would not go in. They were afraid of what might happen. So, the Father borrowed a ladder, climbed up to the window and talked the distraught man out of killing his family. He was at every fire, every tragedy, every accident. He was extraordinary.

My wife and I are not really religious people, we are people of tradition. We wanted a proper marriage that recognized and respected both of our religions. We are people of tolerance. I guess that it was fate that would bring the three of us together. His message was one of tolerance and I suppose that is why the Father gravitated toward us. Even in liberal New York, where almost anything goes, an interfaith marriage is an uncommon occurrence. And so it was, in the midst of his busy days with so many responsibilities he chose to take the time to marry us. The ceremony was not just a job to him – he really believed in what he was doing.

CBS aired a documentary after the attacks. It had been made known to me that images of Father Judge would be part of the video. I couldn't watch. I made sure that I didn't. Yet, the following Tuesday I could avoid the images no longer. As I rode the street car into the city and thumbed through an issue of The National Post, a picture of Father Mychal stared up at me from the page. The last known photograph of the Priest, he was looking skyward. I lost it on the street car. As I cried, fate perhaps once again reached out to me. A woman came to comfort me. To my surprise it was Elizabeth Oughtred, a good friend from my days in New York. How wonderful that she would be in Toronto, on that particular street car, at that particular time to give me friendship and comfort.

I will never forget West 31st Street late at night when New York appeared in its "end of the World" period. Seeing the church and the fire hall and the truck in the middle of the street hit me like a sledge hammer. What a hero he was. Hero is a great word that had become overused. If there is any consolation in his death it is that he died doing what he loved.

If someone were to ask him how he would want to die I am sure he would say that he wanted to die doing his job.

This was not a one off freak event. The United States has enemies. Yet, there does not seem to have been a lot of introspection. This was a brilliantly planned, carefully executed event. The perpetrators were not cowards. There is a lot of hatred toward the US. Why? How can we fix it? There appears to be an arrogance of power that is annoying a lot of people. They must learn humility. They must learn why they are hated. Is it about Israel and Palestine? Is it because of their sense of superiority? They need to learn why and adapt their foreign policy in response. As tragic as this was, there are a lot of deaths in the world because of religious intolerance; just look at the Balkans as one example. The Americans must use their power to create peace.

I want my children to know that Father Mychal brought people together – those who would not otherwise be friends. People from all religions and backgrounds.

I want my children to learn from this and know that we should treat others as we would want to be treated. This is fundamental to all religions.

Because Father Mychal preached the message of tolerance it makes it that much more significant to us to teach that message to our children. Father Mychal will never be a part of their lives in person, but we will make sure that his message is. We will take them to New York and explain it all to them.

My hope is that there would be more priests and nuns like him in the world. I call them practo-Catholics. They get out and work the streets. They express their love and faith by serving others.

Inspired by Father Mychal, we intend to spend the summer in Rome. As a teenager I lived in Italy for four years. This trip is something we have long fantasized about. It probably would never happen had it not been for September 11th. My wife and I work very hard. We spend long hours away from one another and from our children. Our Muslim nanny spends more time with them than we are able! The events of September 11th have caused us to re-evaluate our lives. Life is so short and bad things can happen any time – with little or no warning. So we will spend the summer in Italy, together, as a family, instead of fantasizing, living our dream!

Drawing By: Kimberly Ngan, Age 13, Bayview Hill E. S., Richmond Hill, Ontario

Chapter 21

Building on a Firm Foundation

Alderman Gord Lowe: A City Planner

Gord Lowe is Alderman for Ward 2 of the City of Calgary, and serves on the Calgary Planning Commission. Prior to his election to civic office, Gord held senior positions in Canada's air traffic control system.

Whenever something happens, it's in my nature to look past what is on the surface, to see what lies beneath.

My training and experience in air traffic control were the first to be triggered on September 11ᵗʰ. The phone rang at home: my wife was calling from work to say that an airplane had crashed into the World Trade Center and the information was being carried on TV.

When I tuned in, the second aircraft had just been crashed into the second tower and the TV commentator was speculating about intentional acts. Stunned wonderment at the magnitude of the event was quickly replaced with racing thoughts about air traffic control. What else was going on over New York and elsewhere in the world?

Controllers would have had some warning that these aircraft had diverted from their flight plans. Commercial airliners don't do that without an important reason, generally an on-board emergency: mechanical or human. Other communications options are open to pilots and airline operations centres to alert air traffic controllers, particularly in the case of a hijacking.

Two hijackings was clearly a pattern: how many more loaded aircraft had been commandeered, or were at risk of hijacking? I was certain the air traffic control system across North America was now in real-time communication with the military, co-ordinated through NORAD's command. Tough decisions were being made at the highest levels even as we helplessly watched the twin towers burning.

Every controller in the continent would be checking with every airliner under their control, asking the pilots key questions and verifying responses and flight paths. Airliners that had been hijacked, or where there was some doubt, would be red-circled. The military would be on high alert; fighter interceptors would be scrambled already and in the air above New York and Washington, probably every other major city as well. Orders, we confirmed later, were being issued to these fighter pilots to do the unthinkable: to shoot down one of our own civil airliners, full of innocent passengers and crew.

Instead, air traffic controllers in the north-east listened helplessly as passengers stormed the flight deck of that fourth airliner, and together they dropped off the radar screen, into a field in Pennsylvania.

North American airspace had, by then, been shut down. Air traffic controllers were now doing in real time what they had barely imagined before: re-routing every aircraft, to the nearest designated airfield, in many cases away from strategic urban centres and high probability targets. They did this without knowing how all the planes would even be squeezed onto the aprons and runways of the selected airports, many of them located across Canada. And without knowing how many more of them risked being overpowered by terrorists intent on suicide and mass murder.

The air traffic control system responded admirably that horrible day. Together, the thousands of individuals connected only by headsets and computers defused the risk of more attacks, and handled hundreds of aircraft without further incident. Because it had gone through years of preparation, training and experience.

One ironic preparation had been Y2K—the threat that all our computer and technological systems would come crashing to a halt at midnight, January 1, 2000. Every industry in the world, particularly the air traffic control system, worked through "nightmare scenarios" and worked out in great detail, co-ordinated responses with National Defence. We had no idea at the time, but Y2K helped to prepare us for September 11th, and may well have saved untold lives that day. The system worked, because it's built on a firm foundation.

Since that day, airport and aviation security has undergone a transformation, of course, in Canada, the U.S., and around the world.

Previously, the inconvenience of security arrangements was often regarded as a personal intrusion, and the speedy service of passengers took precedence. In Canada and in North America in general, we have always had a rather cavalier attitude towards personal and group security; kind of a NIMBY ("not in my back yard") response to what we see going on elsewhere. It reminded me of 1919, after the First World War, the "war to end all wars", as North Americans withdrew behind our vast ocean buffers. Surely these would isolate and protect us. They didn't then—the Second World War was the inevitable consequence of our naiveté—and they haven't now. The harsh reality of events elsewhere in the world, but never in Canada or the U.S., had come home to roost.

We are now, sadly, much more aware of the fact that personal security can no longer be taken for granted. I now allow a lot more time when I go to an airport, to deal with the security issue, and stand quietly while the process goes on around me. I look around and feel a little sorry for the folks who don't recognize that times have changed and balk at the new precautions.

It's like deciding to build your house on sand, or on a solid foundation: today's security efforts are taken in order to ensure group safety, and sometimes that means at the expense of personal privacy. Personal, societal and national security are concepts which must be worked at and paid for, by giving up some of our so-called "personal freedoms" that we so cherish: it's the right balance from which we derive strength.

The same thing goes for our cities, particularly our downtown centres. It's a question of seeking the right balance, to ensure a firm foundation.

Will businesses move out of downtowns, out of high-rise towers? Maybe a few will: more businesses will locate their operations in several sites within a city, rather than concentrating them in one location. Operations will be re-deployed throughout the city: the digital world permits that at modest cost, sometimes even at a net savings. Each business has to balance its economies of scale, which increase as operations are concentrated, with emergency preparedness and risk management. So we will see some spreading around.

But downtown will always be downtown, and downtown will be the centre of our cities and our regions. We will continue to build tall office and apartment buildings. Densification of the core of cities is the right answer to preventing the type of urban decay that we've seen in some U.S. cities. In fact, densification has been adopted by leading cities across North America: city centres will be alive and vibrant.

The key to achieving this is people: people living, working and playing in the core, and the downtown core being a destination of choice by those of us who do not live there. The Manhattan downtown and the World Trade Center were not mistakes: indeed, establishing vital city centres is going to be pivotal to social and economic progress in both Canada and the U.S. We need to learn whatever lessons we can from September 11th, but not to retreat or to change course.

If we want to continue to enjoy our open society, we cannot fully protect ourselves. Someday, somewhere, someone will conduct an act which will horrify us as a nation in Canada. But that act should not confine us to our basements. The strongest defence against this type of activity is to carry on. What we can do to dissuade negative activity is to have people and positive activities going on at the very sites those who wish to inflict terror might target. No one wanting to make mischief, regardless of how serious the mischief, wants to conduct that activity under the full glare of the light of day, or the scrutiny of an informed and engaged population.

The dark of night, the absence of people, the lack of attention and response by people who routinely occupy a space or area for whatever the reason creates the climate which facilitates aberrant behaviour. Our task is to create an environment and to foster a population who won't tolerate evil behaviour and who will become involved to prevent it. We need to "take back the night" and defy it happening in our community.

Evil seeks the darkness, and is defeated when exposed to light. If we continue to build our cities on a firm foundation, we shall survive the storms and winds that will inevitably threaten us.

Drawing By: Taylor Carpenter, Grade 5, Wadena Elementary School, Wadena, Saskatchewan

Chapter 22

First In, Last Out

Todd Weiss - A Red Cross Worker

Todd Weiss is a firefighter in Edmonton, a health services technician, who served as a disaster relief volunteer at Ground Zero in New York City for the Red Cross.

I have always been one of the first to enter an apartment, house or office building on fire, so I could relate easily to the firefighters in New York City and Washington on September 11th who rushed into those burning buildings. It's always the same job wherever you go: "the wet stuff on the red stuff" as we say, in our often black firehouse humour.

We were just coming off night shift at Number One Fire Station, downtown Edmonton, on September 11th, with the TV on, when we first found out about it. At first, we couldn't believe it was real; it looked like a movie. It wasn't long before we realized that there would be thousands and thousands dead.

I came home that morning, quietly told my wife, and together we watched the TV news—for hours and hours, in shock.

I've been volunteering for the Red Cross for many years, so phoned them right away to find out what was going on. I went to Red Cross House at noon (the second volunteer to arrive) and helped set up the phone system. We knew that the first need would be communication: people need to know how to contact people, and how to help.

That afternoon, a crew of us went out to the airport and stationed ourselves in Leduc in case we were needed to house passengers from airliners in alternative accommodations. There were almost a dozen planes diverted to Edmonton, but the Airport Authority and airlines were able to arrange enough hotel rooms to accommodate all their passengers. So we headed back to the Red Cross and stationed phones instead.

The phones were ringing like they'd never rung before or since. People wanted to donate money, to donate blood, to volunteer, to help in any way they could. One of the saddest ironies of that day is that so much blood was collected, but none of it was needed at Ground Zero. We waited for the injured, but they were dead. Many people wanted to go and help in New York City. I worked the next two days on phones at Red Cross House, then went back to my regular job with the Fire Department.

Everything had changed at work, too. People were badly rattled; there was a heightened anxiety: people paid attention to every fire alarm, evacuating buildings and crossing the street with every alarm. One lady, scared half to death, called us about a smell in the hallway. It was nothing, but we all took it seriously.

I didn't think there would be any call for me to go to New York, actually. I thought the American Red Cross would handle it completely. But, some two weeks after 9/11, I got a call. The American Red Cross had contacted the Canadian Red Cross in Toronto. They needed some people with specific skills, and requested applications and résumés of qualified volunteers to vet. I had had previous American Red Cross experience during the Mississippi floods, and had managed a flood of Kosovo refugees in Halifax in 1999.

They called back on Friday, and asked me when I could leave. I left on the Saturday, initially the only Red Cross worker from Alberta to serve at Ground Zero. I reported to our headquarters in New York City, one of 21 Canadians among the volunteers. We weren't kept together as a team, though, but each assigned where our skills best fit. But we kept running into each other throughout the city over the coming days.

My initial assignment was as health services disaster relief, manning an aid station which had been situated in Intermediate School 89, or IS89. I was stationed with a nurse from Minnesota at the command post. Together, we dispensed first aid care and medications to whoever came in. Mostly it was army, police and firefighters, who stopped in during their lunch or rest periods.

Firefighters opened up to me, being from Number One Station in Edmonton. They said that there had been almost no organization during the first week, largely disarray because they had lost their command structure. By the second week, they'd put in place a new command structure, and put new restrictions in place. After the second week, two perimeters were established: the outer perimeter for the public, several blocks out, and an inner perimeter around the hot zone itself. Within this inner perimeter, the site itself was closed off to all but New York City firefighters and police.

At the site, FDNY firefighters dug patiently by hand, sifting the debris for human remains. If the remains they found were police, they stopped, and the police went in to dig them out. If they were firefighters, they identified the Fire Station and then stopped. Their own crew shift from that Station came in and brought them out. If it was Port Authority police, same thing, they stopped and Police Authority police came and dug them out. When the going got tough, they brought in ropes and used these to shimmy down voids and gaps at Ground Zero.

Lots of volunteers were shaken up and wide-eyed. One nurse from Canada, about 50 years old, said it was a life-altering experience. Everybody reacts differently depending on their different experience. I found it hit people with office jobs the hardest. Despite its huge scale, I found it had less effect on me, probably because of my firefighting and disaster experience. That made it easier. The hardest part for me wasn't the dead bodies—I've seen more than I can count—but knowing how many firefighters died.

Later, I moved to the Respite Center South, located at the second building in from the impact zone, in the Marriott Financial Center. The first building in, the Marriott Hotel, was evacuated, quiet and empty, having been badly damaged when the South Tower of the World Trade Center fell on it. The Red Cross took over the building, situating registration on the main floor; I manned the First Aid Station on the second floor with nurses from Atlanta and Minnesota. Next to us was a cafeteria, and on the third floor we set up a lounge with lazy boy recliners. Firefighters, police, army, iron workers and crane operators formed our clientele: lots of cold and headache meds, scrapes, sore throats, things like that.

They didn't talk much, that's to be expected. When they did talk, it was usually about September 11th itself: where they were, what they were doing. The best moments for me were when guys would come in and open up. It was good for them to talk with someone, and to get things off their chests.

I stayed in a hotel by Times Square. One day I realized that this could well be the next likely target. I thought for a minute this might not be the best place to stay. Just for a minute though: then I looked at the New Yorkers around me, and moved on.

I walked by the Rockefeller Center, by NBC, and saw lots of emergency vehicles there. Mayor Guiliani was speaking. When I got back to my hotel, I found out they'd found anthrax at NBC.

Ground Zero burned for two months after September 11th. Being a firefighter, you get to recognize certain smells. Here there was a definite smell of burning material, of oil, wood, chairs, but not of dead bodies. Firefighters confirmed to me that they could only smell the dead bodies when they were right there.

One of the positive things about 9/11 is how it caused so many people to sit down and examine their lives and priorities. What am I doing? Am I doing the right things? My own philosophy for many years—even before my dozen years as a firefighter—has been to live life to the fullest. Don't wait for next year, for five years, for retirement. I've seen so many instances where people do just that, they wait, and then they didn't have that time after all. My New York City experience reaffirms that.

It also reaffirms my faith in my fellow man: I met so many good people. You see so many negative aspects of life in my job, that relief work affirms so many good people drop everything to help. I call it a mutual admiration society: volunteers always thanking one another, firefighters thanking the Red Cross, the Red Cross thanking the firefighters. I ran into people all the time, in the street, on the subway, who couldn't believe I'd come from Canada to help out. It was thrilling, almost addictive, to be so appreciated.

A lot of people expect the stereotypical New York City from the 1970's, but the real New York City is so different, so clean, friendly, low crime, safe. I will remember the warmth and hospitality of New Yorkers: of free tours and Broadway plays. I told my wife it was the best and the worst time to go to New

York. Disasters bring the best out of everybody. One of the New Yorkers at the Respite Center said that 9/11 changed the people of New York even more. Will these changes stick for 5 years? For New Yorkers? For us all?

What would I tell the next generation about September 11th? Live your life. Don't wait for tomorrow. How did these problems arise? You have to get educated and you must travel widely. Get as much understanding as you can, and be less prone to prejudice and hate. Be open.

When I got home, I had to face my own kids: a 6 1/2 year old and a 1 1/2 year old. I kept it simple. Yes, it was a terrible thing, a lot of people got hurt. I took my older son to a local fire. I want him to understand why his dad goes away to help, why he has to be the first one in.

I feel very fortunate to have been able to go and help there. Tens of thousands wanted to go but couldn't. I will remember the volunteers, I will remember the lieutenant who came in and sat down, then his crew coming in, exhausted, six firefighters sitting in the first aid room talking day-to-day shop talk, with little details of everyday life. Recovering.

I will remember the firefighter who was working at the Simulation Room where they take school tours. He had been away in Florida on September 11th, but his brother had been here, and was lost at Ground Zero. He came home, went in to work at Ground Zero, and found his brother's helmet. He got very choked up, and took the helmet out to his family. Then he went back to work. That is how he is coping, and relieving his stress by talking about it. He, or someone like him, will be the last one out of Ground Zero.

Drawing By: Heather Nelson, Age 14, Bayview Hill E. S., Richmond Hill, Ontario

Chapter 23

Out of the Mouths of Babes

More Thoughts from Some of Canada's Children

Submissions of written reflections were received from grade school students from across Canada. They are vivid illustrations of how our children deal with September 11th.

Diary Found At Ground Zero

September 11th, 8:30
Dear Diary,

Yes! It is September 11th. I get to go see my dad at work. It is so cool that my dad's law office is at the World Trade Center on the 90th floor. I have never been to the World Trade Center. It think it will be very interesting. There are so many people who work there with interesting jobs. My mom says it will be fun for me.

September 11th, 9:00
Dear Diary,

I am here at the World Trade Center. I am so excited my dad will show me around the Trade Center! I have heard so many stories about it, but I still want to see it.

September 11th, 9:10
Dear Diary,
    I am in my dad's office. His office views the South Tower. Now we will go to the observation deck.
Emily Murphy, Grade 5

"When I watched and heard about all of those innocent people that died in the World Trade Center, I thought that there may be something that I could have done to prevent this tragedy from happening. But when I thought about it over and over I realized that there was absolutely nothing that I could have done except pray."
Anna Lambert, Grade 5

"To this year, to this month, to this day, to this very second, I'm still very sad about all the bombing and fighting going on, but most of all I am very sorry for America. I am still very sad when I talk about it, and then I think how lucky I am to live in Canada, and I feel good that Canada can help America clean up the disaster."
Lisette d'Entremont, Grade 5

"September 11th has made many changes in our lives. Many people wake up each day worrying. Because of the terrorist attack, families have been broken and friends have been lost. Children are scared all day long. People are being checked for bombs, because they want to kill one another. Peace has ended. Army workers are killed for trying to go and see what is going on. Most people in the world have forgotten about peace. They just care about themselves. If everyone in the world would make a bit of effort, each day, to be kind to each other, the World might change."
Marta Cybulsky, Grade 6

"Even though we are a free country it doesn't mean that terrible things can't happen. Let's remember the people who died and hope that terrorism comes to an end; so we can have everlasting peace."

Kristoffer Berg, Grade 5, Wadena Elementary School, Wadena, Saskatchewan

"I learned from September 11th to help people and not to fight. I learned to be careful and not be jealous. I didn't really realize the importance of this until September 11th. Well, now I know so I'll help others and be careful."

Kristin Flanders, Grade 5

Students at Warburg School in Warburg, Alberta answered our questions:

What were your first thoughts and actions?
"Is the world coming to an end or is it going to happen to me and my friends?"
"A lot of people will be hurt."
"I thought it was going to be a world war."
"Are our parents going to war and the terrorists coming here to bomb us?"
"I should be happy with what I have. I am so lucky."
"This will affect Canada."
"This is terrible!"
"Those poor people!"
"How come this is happening to us?"
"I hugged my mom, dad, Nancy, Auntie Jan, sister, and my uncle, cousin and auntie."
"Me and my friends started Pennies 4 Peace — everybody has change in their pockets even a penny."

"I started a campaign called Pennies 4 Peace."
"Oh my God, please make this stop!"

How has it affected you?

"It made me want to see my relatives more."

"I watch the news more."

"Before I was like "What's his problem?", now I'm like "Hey, What's wrong?""

"I have been nicer to my mom, brother, friends and family."

"I became nicer."

"I always make sure I say goodbye to my family."

"I care more."

"Very much I try to make every second fun!"

"We spend more family time and we care more."

"I haven't went into an airplane."

"I became a better person."

"I care more about people and I watch my family more."

"I want to help more."

"I understand more about Remembrance day."

"I am more scared about some things."

"I use my manners more."

What will you remember most?

"I will remember the tall buildings and the people — also the replays."

"I will remember the people dying and the planes crashing."

"I will remember the lawn mower sound when the plane was crashing."

"I will remember the buildings falling."

"I will remember being with my Auntie Jan."

"I will remember watching replays on T.V."

"I will remember it was a terrorist attack."

"I will remember the orange-red-black-gray colored smoke bundling in the air and the thick dark gray smoke going down to the streets of New York."

What do you hope people will learn from this?

"I want every one, including myself, to learn that people should be kind, not mean, you don't deserve that."

"Never go on a plane and never try and kill people on a plane!"

"I want people to know never to fight with people."

"People should have love, peace and freedom and live without terrorism."

"I want people to watch out for suicide people and to help people."

"I hope I will learn not to be like the terrorist and my friends will learn this a lot too."

"I want people to be thankful for what they have."

"I hope that no one will kill other people."

"I want people to be more loving."

"I hope people learn about freedom."

"We must not forget ... even if we want to."

Drawing By: Jennifer Scholten, Grade 5, St. Mary's, Goderich, Ontario

Chapter 24

Hope Restored

Debra Brown: A Traveler

Debra Brown is President of Brown Governance Inc., and is a governance consultant, a frequent speaker at major conferences and seminars and contributor to journals and publications. In addition to her work with BGI, Debra currently serves on two multi-national boards. Her work calls on her to travel away from home a great deal, as was the case on September 11th.

On September 11th, I was in Chicago, in a hotel room by O'Hare airport, sitting at my computer, cramming for a meeting that was to take place later that day. There was a knock at my door, room service was here with my breakfast. He urged my husband and I to turn on our TV: "a plane hit a tower in New York."

How could this possibly be an accident, I asked myself. For a few moments, I tried to convince myself it was, 'though I knew in my heart it probably wasn't. Subconsciously, I wanted to postpone the terrible alternative.

I cried. Then I prayed. When each tower crumbled to the ground, we just held each other and cried for the people trapped inside and their families. It was a horrible feeling, a tearing right through your insides, a dashing of hope.

I was thankful that we were already in Chicago. Our U.S. Air flights the previous evening had been cancelled and we were rebooked on September 11th morning flights via Philadelphia.

But the ground attendant must have seen something in our faces, for she called over to the Air Canada desk and convinced them to take two weary travelers on their direct Ottawa-Chicago flight that night. Timing, as they say, is everything.

So I was safe in a hotel room in Chicago, and didn't think my family would be worried. But my son was worried, so worried that he couldn't stay at work. He heard there were threats against Chicago—including the Sears Tower—and he didn't know exactly where our meeting was. He went home and tracked us down, calling me at the hotel, he was very relieved to speak with me. I felt bad that I hadn't called him first.

My thoughts turned to the day. What does this mean for our meetings? I've got all this work to do to prepare, but it seems so pointless now. Will there even be a meeting? The TV kept distracting me from my computer, but I needed to know what was going on in the world.

The meeting was about evangelism, about helping people learn about, find and know God. Surely this is the solution to the problem, I thought. Hopelessness is a dark place that calls for the light of hope. Here is an even more compelling reason to meet. I decided I must go on working.

I called the meeting chair, Sterling Huston. Sterling is a long-time employee of the Billy Graham Evangelistic Association, and had organized the coalition meeting in Chicago. A lot of people weren't able to make it, however a number had flown in the previous night, and were now grounded here at O'Hare.

Sterling decided we'd go ahead with the strategic planning meeting: it was too important *not* to hold. Because it is really God, who is bigger than the best and the worst of what mankind can do, who is the only hope to solving issues like this.

We ended up extending our meeting to two days from one. It was a good thing, as our work progressed slowly. It was hard to focus. One of the guys kept his laptop on CNN's internet site, pausing to check on news often throughout that long day. Frequently we found ourselves pausing to pray, and to cry. Someone mentioned how ironic it was that the Columbine shootings had happened during the coalition executive's previous strategic planning meeting. Some very trying times, but much more hopeful through the prayers of like-minded people.

The sense of community among those of us grounded together grew as the days stretched out. It wasn't just our colleagues, either, but the entire community of travelers and staff at the hotel.

From the first newsflashes on that fateful morning, the hotel lobby transformed into a gathering place, centered on the TV set high up on the wall facing the check-in desk. Guests like us would wander down from our rooms, glance up at the set and immediately be engaged in a group conversation about the latest news and what it meant. There were a lot of tearful eyes and shaking heads.

Midway through the first morning, staff put up a large white bristol board sign, with block letters in black magic marker: "ALL CHICAGO AIRPORTS CLOSED UNTIL FURTHER NOTICE."

Some people checked out that first day, piling up their luggage at the concierge desk, watching TV and waiting for flights to resume. They checked back in later that night, joining others who had disembarked from planes grounded at O'Hare. The hotel was very good about things. Most of the rooms lay empty all week, since the convention-goers who had booked the hotel for most of the week were no longer able to come. Instead of taking advantage of our situation, and its own economic plight, by charging us higher nightly rates, the hotel manager contacted us and told us she was dropping the rate by a large discount, for our entire stay, however long we needed. Thank you Sheraton!

The sight at O'Hare itself was stunning. None of us could go in there, since its perimeter was completely sealed and patrolled, but we could see the whole panoply from our meeting room atop the hotel. Jetliners stood empty and silent, side-by-side, from one end of the airport to the other: not just on the apron, but on the taxiways and runways as well. Flocks of birds were the only things in flight, indeed the only sound that emanated from this usually bustling spot, all day long. It was eerie.

Each day we expected to leave the following day, based on what the airlines could tell us, but tomorrow took some time to come. A few passengers got word they'd be flying home on Thursday, but not many. We held out hope for Friday, as the continent's air space opened up again and the runways at O'Hare transformed from parking lots to active use. But word came again from U.S. Air: another day in Chicago.

Most of our colleagues had left or were at the airport waiting, so we decided to "play tourist" and hopped on the train into the city center. Strung over every bridge on our route were American flags and home-made banners: "God Bless America", "United We Stand". We rode the L around the loop, took a tour from the Museums to Navy Pier, walked around the main downtown business districts. People were returning to work, to study and to play. Hope was palpable in the eyes of Chicagoans.

On Saturday, our turn came. Traveling was no longer the same. The line-up at check-in was just a foretaste of the rigid security checks. Passengers took this all in stride; we all knew that these steps would have to be in place now, and appreciated the tireless efforts of so many people to restore confidence to flying.

It was a long trip home, with delays both at Chicago and Pittsburgh, but when we stepped off the planes, we all stopped to say "Thank you" to the flight attendants and pilots, but we meant something totally different this week than the week before. Thank you for returning to the skies, for risking your lives to keep us all moving and working. Even now, almost three years later, I still mean that when I thank the flight crew.

Ten days later and it was time for me to fly again. A couple of trips in the meantime had been postponed, as so many organizations paused to take stock. But another board meeting in Chicago was going ahead as scheduled, so I headed back to the planes. I didn't hesitate for a moment. The only way terrorists can succeed is if they change our behaviour, keep us from moving forward. The only way we can succeed is by having hope, and continuing to meet together.

So I boarded the flight. I caught myself looking at each of my fellow travelers, taking particular note of four young Middle Eastern men sitting in different places throughout the mostly empty DC-9. What would I do if something happened? I stopped myself. First, we all know what we'll do if something happens: everyone on the plane will intercede to stop hijackers or terrorists, even if it means our lives. Second, I can't spend my life doubting every Middle Eastern man, profiling people based on their skin colour or looks. That's not a change I want to make.

I have changed since September 11th.

My prayer life has changed. I pray more for world leaders, for the world, for peace, for the next generation, than I did before. My prayers are less selfish, more others-focused, more global in scope.

I am more determined now to pursue my calling: those things I have a passion for and that can make a difference in the world. And more determined to find balance between family and work.

I have more faith. My faith has deepened as I watch the response of leaders, and children. As I watch people reach out spiritually and in unconditional love to strangers, my faith has grown. As I see God work good in spite of evils, my faith has strengthened.

I am more hopeful now than before September 11th, even though that might sound strange. I've seen good prevail. I've seen hope in the eyes of survivors, and families of survivors, and those who lead us. I've seen hopefulness in how children have responded—in actions and giving, in poems, in stories—and that gives me hope for the future.

I love more, in greater depth, and I'm much more determined to love, whether family, or neighbours, or people I don't know or understand. I choose to love them first and then get to know and understand them second.

My desire for the next generation is that they would learn to have faith, to have hope and to love. By love I mean learning how to really love, and to understand the depths of love—love isn't just a surface emotion, but a choice, reaching down deep even to the point of loving your enemies. By faith, not just a surface faith, but reaching out to God, really understanding what you believe and why. By hope, not just a surface hope, but true optimism: in love, because of faith, we can reach out to the future with real hope, not empty aspirations.

Faith, hope and love: so much has been written about them, yet the bottom line is that we are called on to respond from the depths of them. This book is my personal response of faith, hope and love.

For ever, I will remember the moment I first saw those pictures on the TV screen; they are etched in my memory. But I will remember most the way the world came together over a single event in history, as good prevailed over evil.

I will remember the church services, from the Chicagoans who crowded into local churches for round-the-clock vigils to the national service at which the Reverend Billy Graham spoke later that same week. I will remember spontaneous and unfettered public prayer, from the President and White House staff praying on the White House lawn to the members of Congress standing on the steps of the Capitol singing a hymn. I will remember people, Americans and Canadians, being courageous despite the evil coming against them. Courageous leadership is what brought the world together.

I will also remember those who died. That's why I'm writing this book. I—we—can't forget those people who lost their lives, that day we all lost much of our innocence. In remembering them, we shall leave a legacy of peace for the future. In spite of everything that day, I had the overwhelming sense that God knew the mourning and loss the world was feeling, and He grieved with us. And although it seemed out of control, in God's economy it was always in control: I will remember that God knew the evil choices of men and yet in His sovereignty He would ensure everything in the end was going to be O.K. That terrible day, I knew in my heart that good would once again prevail over evil and my hope was restored.

As I close out this book, I am reminded of the many "Orange Alerts" the United States has issued in response to imminent security threats against their nation and people. My hope is we will learn the lessons of September 11th and never forget the application of those lessons. For wouldn't it be wonderful to have a day and a time in the near future when orange is but a colour we teach our children and our grandchildren and Alert is a quiet station in the Canadian north.

"Oh this it is hard to see, there is always hope for you and me – and peace."
Drawing by: Michelle, Age 7, Bandec Peak School, Bragg Creek, Alberta

ORANGE ALERT

Acknowledgement

The authors would like to acknowledge with deep appreciation the openness and willingness of the interviewees and other contributors to this book. In many cases this involved opening up old wounds, but we hope the result will be deeper healing.

Go to **www.orangealert.ca** to view the full colour artwork of all drawings found in this book.

ISBN 141203717-4